Vietnam War
Battles and Leaders

Vietnam War
Battles and Leaders

AARON R. MURRAY, EDITOR

DK Publishing, Inc.

LONDON, NEW YORK, MUNICH,
MELBOURNE, AND DELHI

DK PUBLISHING, INC.
Editors Madeline Farbman and Elizabeth Hester
Senior Designer Tai Blanche
Assistant Managing Art Editor Michelle Baxter
Senior Editor Beth Sutinis
Creative Director Tina Vaughan
Jacket Art Director Dirk Kaufman
Production Manager Chris Avgherinos
DTP Coordinator Milos Orlovic

MEDIA PROJECTS INC.
Executive Editor Carter Smith
Editor Aaron R. Murray
Writer Stuart Murray
Project Manager James A. Burmester
Consultants Clifford J. Rogers, United States
Military Academy; Steve R. Waddell,
United States Military Academy
Designer Laura Smyth, Smythtype
Cartography Ron Toelke, Rob Stokes
Picture Researcher Erika Rubel
Researcher Aimee Kraus
Copy Editor Glenn Novak

First American Edition, 2004
04 05 06 07 08 10 9 8 7 6 5 4 3 2 1

Published in the United States
by DK Publishing, Inc.
375 Hudson Street
New York, New York 10014

A catalog record for this book is available
from the Library of Congress.

ISBN 0-7566-0771-X (pb)
ISBN 0-7566-0770-1 (hc)

Reproduced by Colourscan, Singapore
Printed and bound in China by
South China Printing Co., Ltd.

Discover more at
www.dk.com

*Halftitle: U.S. helicopter takes off from Duc Co
Special Forces camp, 1965. Title page: South
Vietnamese troops on patrol, 1961.*

CONTENTS

U.S. ARMY
SERVICE MEDALS

VIET CONG FLAG

AMERICAN M-16 ASSAULT RIFLE

U.S. ARMY SHOULDER PATCH

VIET CONG KNIFE

FRENCH INDOCHINA CONFLICT

World War II weakened the European powers and shook the foundations of their empires. As a result, many colonies began to fight for independence, including the peoples of Southeast Asia.

LAST EMPEROR
Vietnamese emperor Bao Dai reviews French and colonial paratroopers during the First Indochina War. French officers and officials follow the emperor, who was considered no more than a puppet ruler controlled by France.

Japan occupied the Indochina Peninsula of Southeast Asia during World War II. Close to defeat by early 1945, Japan withdrew many of her troops from Indochina to protect her homeland. When the Japanese left, the French retook Indochina, which France had colonized for almost 70 years.

The Vietnamese people of eastern Indochina had fought for generations against French rule. In 1946, their struggle for independence continued in what was called the First Indochina War (1946–1954). An alliance of Vietnamese nationalists and Communists led by revolutionary

CONTAINMENT POLICY
President Truman, right, confers with Secretary of State Dean Acheson, who urged supporting the French in Indochina to stop Communist expansion.

Ho Chi Minh raised an army to fight the French. Ho declared Vietnam to be independent. He won support from Communist leaders Mao Zedong of the People's Republic of China and Joseph Stalin of the Soviet Union.

The United States opposed political movements that had strong Communist backing. America did not want a Communist Vietnam. President Harry S. Truman and later President Dwight D. Eisenhower believed that if Vietnam were taken over by Ho's Communists, then nearby countries also would fall under Communist control. This became known as the "domino theory," which compared small countries to a row of dominoes standing on end. If one domino falls, it knocks over the next, which knocks over the next, and so on.

America gave France immense financial and military aid to oppose Ho's forces. The French named Bao Dai, the European-educated emperor of Vietnam, as official ruler of the country. The revolutionaries refused to accept him, however. Fighting raged for almost nine years, until the French were defeated in 1954 and forced to withdraw from Vietnam.

SOVIET PREMIER
Joseph Stalin's Soviet Union was the second most powerful nation after the United States. The Soviets supported the Communist-led ietnamese independence movement.

The peace agreement between France and the Vietnamese nationalists divided Vietnam into North and South. The North was led by Ho and the Communists, the South by Vietnamese who favored French rule and opposed Communism. The peace terms stated that the Vietnamese people were to vote to decide which government was to rule all Vietnam. The United States opposed elections, fearing the Communists would win and take over all Vietnam. In 1955, the Americans helped create the Republic of Vietnam (RVN) in the South, led by President Ngo Dinh Diem. The stage was set for the Second Indochina War.

HO IN FRANCE
Vietnamese leader Ho Chi Minh arrives in Paris in 1946 to negotiate the independence of his country. The French did not cooperate, and instead set up a separate government in southern Vietnam. Ho soon returned home to wage war.

D uring the 1950s, the United States followed a policy of anti-communist "containment"—the effort to stop Communist expansion everywhere in the world. Americans believed North Vietnam must be "contained" to keep Communism from spreading across Southeast Asia. In 1957, Communist-led Vietnamese nationalists set out to defeat the Republic of Vietnam (RVN), as South Vietnam was named. They aimed to unite North and South and establish one Vietnamese nation.

Backed by military aid from the Soviet Union and Communist China, the North Vietnamese Democratic Republic of Vietnam (DRV) organized a guerrilla war gainst President Diem. America aided Diem, even though his government was oppressive and corrupt. At least it was solidly anti-

PRESIDENTIAL INAUGURATION
Containing Communism was on Kennedy's mind during his 1961 inauguration in Washington, D.C. He considered South Vietnam a "cornerstone of the Free World" and "a test of American responsibility and determination."

communist. By 1960, several thousand American military advisors were in Vietnam, training government troops and sometimes leading them in battle.

President John F. Kennedy increased the number of American troops in Vietnam to 16,000 by 1963. Yet, even with American support, Diem could not defeat his stubborn enemy. Early in November of that year,

GREETING THE TROOPS
President Johnson shakes hands with U.S. soldiers during a surprise visit to Vietnam in 1966. He said he would "stand firm," although 6,000 Americans had already died in the war.

ANTIAIRCRAFT GUNNERS
Air defense soldiers look for U.S. warplanes in the skies above the North Vietnamese capital, Hanoi, in 1969. More bombs rained on Vietnam than were dropped during all of World War II.

and the war became more ferocious. Antiwar opposition was growing ever more widespread.

By 1971, the Army of the Republic of Vietnam (ARVN) was taking more military responsibility, and U.S. troops were being withdrawn. Nixon increased bombing while negotiating peace with Hanoi. Terms were signed in 1973, and the last U.S. forces withdrew. More than 58,000 Americans and at least 3 million Vietnamese had lost their lives. In 1975, North Vietnam invaded South Vietnam, which fell in April. Vietnam was unified as one Communist nation, ending the Second Indochina War, better known to Americans as the Vietnam War.

rebellious South Vietnamese generals overthrew Diem. Later that month, Kennedy was assassinated, and Vice President Lyndon B. Johnson became president. Johnson began heavy bombing campaigns and sent tens of thousands of troops to Vietnam.

In 1968, more than 535,000 Americans were in Southeast Asia, but the struggle dragged on. Meanwhile, opposition to the war grew stronger in the United States. Johnson was disappointed at his failure in Vietnam and declined to run for another term as president. Richard M. Nixon was elected,

DEADLY MINE
Antipersonnel mines detonated when stepped on or when a trigger wire was tripped. One in 10 American deaths was the result of booby traps or mines.

FOOT-SLOGGING
These First Cavalry soldiers watch the ground to avoid booby traps such as sharpened stakes in covered holes or hidden explosives.

CONFLICT IN SOUTHEAST ASIA

1946–1964

SEPTEMBER 1945 Japan surrenders, ending World War II • Ho Chi Minh declares Vietnam independent • First Indochina War begins

AUGUST 1950 U.S. Military Assistance Advisory Group set up to aid French

MAY 1954 Fall of Dien Bien Phu, final defeat of French in Indochina

OCTOBER 1955 Ngo Dinh Diem becomes president of Republic of Vietnam (South)

JANUARY 1963 Army of the Republic of Vietnam (ARVN) units defeated at Ap Bac

NOVEMBER Military coup overthrows Diem • President John F. Kennedy assassinated • Lyndon B. Johnson becomes president

AUGUST 1964 Gulf of Tonkin incident • U.S. Senate passes Gulf of Tonkin Resolution • Air strikes on North Vietnam begin

1965

MARINES WATCH ARTILLERY STRIKES ON ENEMY POSITIONS IN 1965.

FEBRUARY Viet Cong (VC) guerrillas attack U.S. base at Pleiku

MARCH First Marine combat troops deployed to Vietnam • Air campaign Operation Rolling Thunder begins, lasts until October 1968

APRIL LBJ decides to increase forces in Vietnam to 33,000 troops

JUNE Battle at Dong Xoai: Special Forces, sailors, and South Vietnamese against VC

JULY LBJ decides to increase force to 125,000

AUGUST Operation Starlite, first major U.S. ground offensive • Operation Market Time attacks enemy supply routes

NOVEMBER Battle of Ia Drang Valley • Air cavalry assault at Landing Zone X-Ray • Pentagon calls for 400,000 troops in 1966

1966

U.S. INFANTRY EVACUATE THEIR WOUNDED.

JANUARY LBJ resumes air campaign after a pause in bombing North Vietnam in an unsuccessful attempt to bring enemy to negotiations

MARCH VC and North Vietnamese Army (NVA) troops destroy U.S. Special Forces base in A Shau Valley • Anti-government Buddhist demonstrations result in riots and clashes between civilians and South Vietnamese troops

JUNE U.S. air raids on Hanoi and Haiphong destroy much of North Vietnam's fuel supplies

AUGUST Australian troops win Battle of Long Tan

SEPTEMBER–NOVEMBER Operation Attleboro drives VC force across Cambodian border

1967

JANUARY Operation Bolo, air campaign • Operation Cedar Falls—U.S. and ARVN troops attack "Iron Triangle"

FEBRUARY Operation Junction City—U.S. and ARVN strike north of Saigon

APRIL Major antiwar demonstrations in New York and San Francisco

MAY Defense secretary Robert McNamara recommends cutting back on bombing

JULY Marines battle NVA at Con Thien • McNamara visits Saigon, agrees to increase of 55,000 troops

AUGUST Bombing of North intensified

OCTOBER Major antiwar march on Washington, D.C.; more than 50,000 protesters • Bombing of Hanoi and Haiphong increases

NOVEMBER–DECEMBER Battle of Dak To, fierce clash between U.S. and North Vietnamese troops • McNamara resigns as secretary of defense, objecting to increased bombing

1968

A PARATROOPER MANS A MACHINE GUN
IN THE BATTLE OF DAK TO.

JANUARY–FEBRUARY NVA-VC Tet Offensive

JANUARY–APRIL Siege of Khe Sanh; marines fight off determined enemy attacks

MARCH My Lai massacre: U.S. infantry kill more than 300 civilians • LBJ declares he will not run for president

JULY Phoenix program begins: CIA-run campaign to eliminate leading VC supporters in South Vietnamese countryside

OCTOBER LBJ announces end to Operation Rolling Thunder

NOVEMBER Richard M. Nixon elected president

1969

JANUARY–MARCH Preliminary meetings held in Paris for future peace talks • Marines attack NVA base area in Da Krong Valley near Laotian border in Operation Dewey Canyon • Paratroopers launch a followup assault through the valley in March in Operation Massachusetts Striker

MARCH Operation Menu: secret bombing of Cambodia • U.S. government begins policy of "Vietnamization": ARVN to bear more defense burden • U.S. troops at maximum strength, 536,000

MAY 101st Airborne fights the Battle of Ap Bia Mountain, nicknamed "Hamburger Hill"

ANTIWAR PROTESTERS MARCH ON INDEPENDENCE
AVENUE IN WASHINGTON, D.C.

JUNE Nixon announces that 25,000 troops will be withdrawn from Vietnam later in the year; regular troop reductions will continue thereafter

AUGUST U.S. Secretary of State Henry Kissinger meets privately with North Vietnamese representative in Paris

SEPTEMBER Ho Chi Minh dies in Hanoi

1970–1971

APRIL–MAY 1970 U.S. invades Cambodia

APRIL Ohio National Guard fires on antiwar demonstrators at Kent State University, killing 4 students and wounding 10

JUNE Senate repeals Gulf of Tonkin Resolution

JANUARY–FEBRUARY 1971 U.S. conducts Operation Dewey Canyon II to clear routes near Laotian border

FEBRUARY–APRIL ARVN troops strike across Laotian border in Operation Lam Son 719

MARCH Prince Sihanouk is overthrown by his anti-communist defense minister, General Lon Nol, opening the way for a U.S. invasion to strike at NVA supply routes and bases in Cambodia

NOVEMBER U.S. troops number 139,000

1972–1975

U.S. AND VIETNAMESE DELEGATES SIGN THE
PEACE AGREEMENT IN PARIS.

FEBRUARY 1972 Nixon visits China, meets Mao Zedong

MARCH–JULY NVA opens new offensives

MAY–OCTOBER Nixon orders Operation Linebacker, massive bombing campaign against North Vietnam

DECEMBER Operation Linebacker II renews bombing, targets Hanoi and Haiphong

JANUARY 1973 Paris Peace Agreement signed by U.S., North Vietnam, South Vietnam, and VC: U.S. military presence in Vietnam ends 60 days later

JANUARY–APRIL 1975 NVA offensive closes with fall of Saigon on April 30, ending the Second Indochina War

THE VIETNAM WAR

CHINA

The peace terms that ended the First Indochina War (1946–1954) between France and Vietnamese nationalists drew a dividing line between North and South Vietnam. A Demilitarized Zone (DMZ) was established at the 17th parallel, where neither side was permitted to station troops. Arms and supplies were sent from North Vietnam through the jungles of Laos and Cambodia to antigovernment guerrillas in South Vietnam. Government military bases were established throughout the South to fight the guerrillas and keep control of the cities. By the early 1960s, American forces were led by the Military Assistance Command, Vietnam (MACV). South Vietnam was divided into four military regions, numbered I–IV. MACV built major military bases at Da Nang and around Saigon, with the main U.S. naval base at Cam Ranh Bay. The air war against North Vietnam and enemy forces operating in South Vietnam was launched from ten main air bases and from aircraft carriers in the South China Sea. Most South Vietnamese cities and towns were sites of major battles, and strategic American positions and military bases came under frequent attack.

LUANG PRABANG

L

TH

N
W E
S

INDIAN
OCEAN

BANGKOK

A GUNNER FIRES FROM A
U.S. NAVY HELICOPTER.

Red River

NORTH VIETNAM

CHINA

DIEN BIEN PHU

HANOI ★

HAIPHONG

XIENG KHOUANG

THANH HOA

GULF OF TONKIN

HAINAN (CHINA)

VINH

Mekong River

ENTIANE

DONG HAI

NAKHON PHANOM

JHAKHEK

DEMILITARIZED ZONE (DMZ)

Hickory Hill

QUANG TRI

SAVANNAKHET

KHE SANH

HUÉ

DA NANG

I CORPS

CHU LAI

Leghorn

QUANG NGAI

UBON

Central Highlands

Mekong River

DAK TO

KONTUM

PHU CAT

PLEIKU

QUI NHON

CAMBODIA

STUNG TRENG

II CORPS

SIEM REAP

BAN ME THUOT

TUY HOA

ATTAMBANG

Tonle Sap

KRATIE

NHA TRANG

KOMPONG CHAM

SOUTH VIETNAM

Cam Ranh Bay

PHNOM PENH ★

THAN SON NHUT

PHAN RANG

Mekong River

III CORPS

BIEN HOA

Camp Yen The

KOMPONG SOM (SIHANOUKVILLE)

Nui Ta Bac

SAIGON

VUNG TO

BIN THUY

AP BAC

Mekong Delta

SOUTH CHINA SEA

CAN THO

GULF OF THAILAND

IV CORPS

KIEN LAM

▲ U.S. AIRBASE

▲ STRATEGIC HILLTOP

━ U.S. CORPS BOUNDARIES

● CITIES AND TOWNS

★ NATIONAL CAPITALS

13

Vietnam's Warrior Spirit Defeats France

The people of Indochina have often fought for freedom from foreign rule. The Vietnamese people's wars with Chinese invaders raged over 2,000 years of Indochinese history.

In the late 1800s, France colonized Indochina but had to put down frequent rebellions by the Vietnamese people. In the early twentieth century, many Vietnamese nationalists became Communists, especially those who were educated in Europe. They wanted a country built on the principles that had established the Soviet Union after World War I (1914–1918). This meant eliminating capitalism and ending the French colonial system.

In World War II (1939–1945), Japan captured Indochina. Now, Vietnamese nationalists fought Japanese occupiers. The rebel army was known as "Vietminh"—a term taken from the

VIETMINH WOMEN
Female fighters played an important part in the Vietnamese struggle for independence in the 1940s. These officers stand before their company of spear-carrying women, including children, assembled at muster. The unit's commander, center, wears an army-issue pistol, holster belt, and jacket.

August 1945	September 1945	December 1946	March 1949
World War II ends	Ho Chi Minh proclaims Vietnamese independence from France	Vietminh attack French in Hanoi	French make Bao Dai puppet head of state
Emperor Bao Dai gives up the throne		First Indochina War begins	

Vietnamese name for the Vietnam Independence League. These guerrilla fighters were aided by American advisors who provided them with weapons and training.

With the defeat of Japan in 1945, France reclaimed her Indochina colonies and sent in troops. This touched off another rebellion by the nationalists, who were led by Communist revolutionary Ho Chi Minh. Continuing the age-old struggle against foreigners, Ho's rebels organized and trained military units in the villages. The long Vietnamese tradition of defeating more powerful enemies made the Vietminh believe that they could achieve final victory.

Known as the First Indochina War, this bloody conflict lasted nine years, ending with a crushing French defeat at Dien Bien Phu in May 1954.

FRENCH TROOPS ON PATROL
Weary soldiers of the French colonial army wade across a muddy river on campaign in the First Indochina War (1946–1954). A soldier has slipped and fallen, weighed down by his heavy knapsack.

IN TRAINING

Early in 1945, the Japanese took complete control of Indochina and imprisoned French troops and administrators. Now the Vietnamese rebels concentrated on fighting the Japanese occupying forces. Soon, American advisors from the secret Office of Strategic Services (OSS) arrived to train and arm Ho Chi Minh's forces at hidden camps. The Vietminh were effective guerrilla fighters against the Japanese, who were losing the wider war in the Pacific. The first American to die in Vietnam was an OSS officer, killed in 1945 while operating with the Vietminh.

LEARNING FROM AMERICANS
An American OSS officer at a base camp in the jungles of northern Vietnam teaches anti-Japanese Vietminh fighters how to throw hand grenades. The Vietminh quickly became skilled fighters.

June 1950	May 1954	August 1954	October 1954
President Truman sends U.S. troops to fight Communist forces in Korea	Dien Bien Phu falls to the Vietminh	Geneva Accords divide Vietnam into North and South	French leave Hanoi
The Korean War begins	Geneva Conference begins	Ngo Dinh Diem becomes leader of South Vietnam	President Eisenhower provides military aid to Diem's regime

VIETNAMESE RISE UP

With the defeat of Japan in 1945, many Vietnamese were ready for independence. Ho Chi Minh hoped the United States would support a free Vietnam, which he promised would be a democracy. On September 2, 1945, Ho proclaimed the Democratic Republic of Vietnam (DRV), based in Hanoi. Emperor Bao Dai gave up his throne and joined Ho's government as "supreme counselor."

Meanwhile, the French gave the Hanoi government limited independence, but kept control of its finances. Also, France was allowed to station troops in the republic as defense against any foreign attack. There was, however, much hostility between the French and Hanoi's Vietminh soldiers. In 1946, after several clashes, mostly brought on by

the French, this hostility erupted into open warfare. The outgunned Vietminh retreated from the cities to continue the fight. They reorganized under Ho and self-taught general Vo Nguyen Giap. The struggle intensified as more French troops arrived and the Vietminh became a better fighting force. The French controlled the cities, but the rebels held much of the countryside.

Star and number on wooden handle

ARMY KNIFE
This soldier's knife is typical of the modest equipment used by Vietnamese resistance forces. It has a simple design and is cheap to manufacture. The handle bears the symbol and number of a military unit.

THE PEOPLE'S GENERAL
General Vo Nguyen Giap, in civilian clothes, reviews Vietminh troops in 1951. An ally of Ho Chi Minh, Giap created the Vietminh army in 1944. He led it, and later the NVA (North Vietnamese Army), through the Indochina wars.

Losses First Indochina War	
Vietminh:	250,000 civilians killed
French/Allies:	94,581 killed/missing, 78,127 wounded

Fighting spread, and by 1949 France had reinstated Bao Dai as emperor. They hoped he could be chief of state and help negotiate peace. Bao Dai had no such influence over the Vietnamese, and conflict continued. That same year, China was taken over by Mao Zedong's Communist Party. Then, in 1950, the Communist North Koreans invaded South Korea, starting the Korean War. Now the United States urged France to defeat the Vietminh so that Indochina would not fall to the Communists.

INDOCHINA
France ruled three colonies—Vietnam, Laos, and Cambodia—as the Indochinese Union. Hanoi was the main city of northern Vietnam, and Saigon in the south was the leading center for commerce and French cultural influence.

FRENCH CONTROLLED INDOCHINA
VIETMINH CONTROLLED AREAS, 1946-1954

THE LEADERSHIP

FRANCE AND THE U.S. considered hereditary emperor Bao Dai the Vietnamese head of state. He had little authority, however. French general Jean de Lattre de Tassigny was a key commander and high commissioner for Indochina. Ho and Giap determined the Vietminh strategy.

BAO DAI (1913-1997)
Emperor since 1925, Bao Dai was educated in France and lived abroad until 1932. Modern and stylish, he was known as the "Playboy Emperor." Bao Dai is shown in Paris in 1954, as France prepares to leave Vietnam.

"Should you reestablish a French administration here, it will not be obeyed. Every village will be a nest of resistance...."
—Bao Dai to French government

"[We would welcome] a million American soldiers...but no French."
—Ho Chi Minh, to an OSS agent

HO CHI MINH (1890-1969)
Ho studies maps at his secret headquarters in the caves of Cao Bang Province in 1951. Ho's years of leadership made him Vietnam's most important founding father.

LOSS OF AN EMPIRE

The French were successful in the early years of the First Indochina War as they drove the Vietminh deep into the jungles and mountains. Yet Giap and Ho kept up their resistance and began receiving aid from Communist China. Now the Vietminh went on the offensive, capturing outposts and wiping out military columns on the roads.

By 1953, French casualties numbered more than 90,000. Although Vietminh losses were far higher, Giap accepted heavy casualties as long as he weakened the enemy. French general Henri Navarre wanted to bring about a major battle with the Vietminh. He was sure his troops would decisively defeat them. In early 1954, he positioned some 15,000 soldiers at Dien Bien Phu—in the middle of Vietminh territory. The French were commanded by Colonel Christian de Castries. Giap soon encircled De Castries with 55,000 men and hundreds of artillery pieces that pounded the French for 55 days. French strongpoints fell one by one. When their airfield was destroyed,

THE LEADERSHIP

BLAME FOR DEFEAT AT DIEN BIEN PHU lies with General Navarre, who underestimated Giap. Navarre did not expect artillery to appear on hills overlooking the base. Credit goes to Vietminh commanders who organized thousands of men to drag the heavy guns into position.

CHRISTIAN DE CASTRIES (1901-1991)
Colonel de Castries studies maps in his besieged Dien Bien Phu headquarters bunker. A highly decorated, 52-year-old commando and cavalry officer, he was a tank officer and a daredevil pilot. De Castries survived the battle and retired in 1969.

"Now we can see it clearly— the light at the end of the tunnel."

—Navarre, predicting victory in Vietnam

"...strike to win, strike only when success is certain. If it is not, then do not strike."

—Giap, describing his strategy

PRECISE PLANNING
At his jungle headquarters, Ho Chi Minh, left, consults with commanders studying a model of French defenses at Dien Bien Phu. At right is General Vo Nguyen Giap, who won the battle.

the only route of escape was closed. At last, on May 7, de Castries's headquarters bunker was taken, and the French surrendered.

Approximately 2,000 French and 8,000 Vietminh died at Dien Bien Phu. More than 10,800 French were marched off to harsh prison camps, where only 3,290 survived.

Peace terms were signed on July 20 in Geneva, Switzerland. The "Geneva Accords" granted independence to French Indochina and gave the Vietminh control of Vietnam north of the 17th parallel. Further, the Vietnamese were to hold elections within two years to decide who would rule all Vietnam. The United States refused to endorse the Geneva Accords.

EMPIRE LOST
Dien Bien Phu lay in mountains on the Vietnam-Laotian border. Vietminh victory there in 1954 cost France its Indochina colonies, which were granted independence.

FRENCH TERRITORY AFTER DIEN BIEN PHU

Eisenhower's government wanted a democratic South Vietnam with a pro-American ruler.

VIETNAMESE FLAG
The national flag of Vietnam bears a gold star on a red background. The flags of the Soviet Union and Communist China also use the color red—symbolizing revolution—with gold designs.

SIGNALING POSSESSION
Vietminh soldiers wave their flag to show they occupy the headquarters bunker of the French commander at the center of the fortified French base. The bunker's capture on May 7 ended a siege of 55 days.

Losses	
Vietminh:	8,000 killed, 12,000 wounded
French:	3,000 killed, 8,000 wounded

Vietnam's War Becomes an American Conflict

The Eisenhower administration opposed any unification vote that might create a Communist-ruled Vietnam. Meanwhile, thousands of former Vietminh fighters living in the South prepared to fight again.

In 1955, the United States backed Ngo Dinh Diem, a Roman Catholic politician. Diem named himself president of the Republic of Vietnam (RVN) in the South and removed Bao Dai as head of state. While America financed and trained the South Vietnamese army, Diem began repressing communist suspects and opponents of the government. The former Vietminh fighters were in open rebellion by late 1957. They attacked government troops and murdered local leaders they mistrusted.

In 1960, anti-government groups formed the National Liberation Front (NLF) to fight Diem. His government labeled NLF members "Viet Cong" (VC),

MONKS PROTEST OPPRESSION
Buddhist monks lead a demonstration in Saigon, calling for the government to stop mistreating members of their faith. Approximately 70 percent of the population was Buddhist, and they organized strong opposition to Diem's mainly Catholic government.

January 1955	April 1956	May 1959	December 1960
Diem becomes president of South Vietnam

Republic of (South) Vietnam is founded | Last French troops leave South Vietnam | Construction begins on the Ho Chi Minh Trail | National Liberation Front (NLF) is founded to coordinate the war in the South |

meaning Vietnamese Communists. NLF supplies and fighters came from the North by following a jungle route called the Ho Chi Minh Trail. The VC became ever more effective, defeating the army at Ap Bac early in 1963.

Other troubles developed for Diem as Buddhists protested persecution by his pro-Catholic government. Also, ambitious South Vietnamese generals wanted Diem's power. They overthrew and executed him in November, placing a general in office. President Kennedy died later that same month, killed by an assassin's bullet.

In August 1964, the U.S. Navy claimed the North Vietnamese attacked a warship in the Gulf of Tonkin. Congress quickly passed a resolution that gave President Johnson broad powers to expand U.S. forces and widen the war in Vietnam.

ARVN INFANTRY ATTACK
American-equipped and trained South Vietnamese soldiers advance through the swampy marshlands of the Mekong Delta in search of Viet Cong in 1961. American Special Forces officers sometimes led ARVN units, whose own officers were often incompetent.

TWO ASSASSINATIONS

After Kennedy was elected president in 1960, American military advisors in Vietnam increased in number. In 1963, more than $500 million in aid went to South Vietnam, including the most modern equipment. The Kennedy administration was unhappy, however, with Diem's tyrannical rule. The U.S. ambassador to South Vietnam, Henry Cabot Lodge, advised supporting several generals who were plotting against Diem. Few in Washington objected early that November when Diem was overthrown and murdered. Then, on November 22, Kennedy was assassinated during a visit to Dallas.

A FATAL DAY
Moments before the assassination, President Kennedy and First Lady Jacqueline Kennedy ride in a motorcade through Dallas. Doubt remains over whether Kennedy would have widened the war in Vietnam.

November 1961	January 1963	November	August 1964
President Kennedy sends military aid and advisors to South Vietnam	Battle of Ap Bac	Diem is overthrown President Kennedy is assassinated	Congress passes Gulf of Tonkin Resolution

OSS TO CHOPPERS

The first American military advisors to Vietnam were OSS agents in World War II. After the war, the OSS was changed into a new spying operation: the Central Intelligence Agency (CIA). The first military advisors to the Diem regime were CIA agents. Based in the South, they created secret sabotage units to destroy the North Vietnamese transportation system and slow down rebuilding from the First Indochina War.

In 1954, the Eisenhower administration promised Diem $100 million in aid. Although South Vietnam was very poor and needed economic help, most of this aid was for a military buildup. The U.S. established the Military Assistance Advisory Group (MAAG) for South Vietnam in 1956. American military advisors trained the ARVN and taught them how to use weapons. Advisors were not to take part in combat. As the VC insurgency intensified, however, advisors were often involved in fighting. The first American advisors were killed in action in 1959.

THE LEADERSHIP

IN 1954, CIA AGENT Colonel Edward Landsdale set up the Saigon Military Mission to undermine North Vietnam and back Diem. Landsdale's "dirty tricks" helped Diem win the presidency. General Paul D. Harkins led U.S. military advisors until 1964.

MAXWELL TAYLOR (1901–1987)
President Kennedy's military advisor, General Taylor was head of the Joint Chiefs of Staff from 1962 to 1964. A World War II hero and former commander of the Eighth Army in Korea, Taylor recommended increasing U.S. military involvement in Southeast Asia.

"[South Vietnam] is not an excessively difficult or unpleasant place to operate."
—Taylor, advising Kennedy to increase U.S. forces

NGO DINH DIEM (1901–1963)
A wealthy member of the Catholic ruling class under the French, Diem was a staunch anti-communist nationalist. As South Vietnam's president (1954–1963), Diem was harsh and repressive, and his government was corrupt. ARVN generals mutinied and murdered him in November 1963.

"I have tried to do my duty.... I am trying to reestablish order."
—Diem, telling U.S. ambassador Henry Cabot Lodge about the generals' mutiny

The years from 1954 to 1964 were known as the "Advisory Phase." In the late 1950s, military advisors numbered 700. President Kennedy's administration realized the Diem government could not defeat the VC without more help, and the number of advisors rose to 1,200 by 1962. Now the United States formed a new headquarters group, known as Military Assistance Command, Vietnam (MACV). The total number of advisors jumped to 16,000 in 1963. American pilots began flying combat operations supporting the ARVN, and American helicopter crews ferried ARVN troops into action, backing them with firepower. The U.S. moved ever deeper into the Southeast Asia conflict.

COMMUNIST-HELD AREAS

MAIN HO CHI MINH TRAIL

ROUTE TO SAIGON
Much of the VC activity during the "Advisory Phase" of the Vietnam conflict was around Saigon. The direct route for moving men and supplies toward the South Vietnam capital ran along the border in Laos.

JUNGLE HAT
Soldiers often preferred comfortable soft hats instead of bulky steel helmets. Jungle hats in camouflage colors helped soldiers remain concealed in action.

Losses 1961–1965

U.S.:	1,864 killed, 7,337 wounded

MILITARY ADVISOR
ARVN troops learn how to set up and fire a 60-mm mortar under the guidance of Captain Alfred H. McKeown in 1963. American soldiers often led ARVN troops into battle during the "Advisory Phase" of the Vietnam conflict.

A TURNING POINT

Growing American support did not always persuade ARVN commanders to fight harder. Diem's officer corps was corrupt. Senior ARVN commanders too often looked for the Americans to do the hardest fighting. Further, Diem did not honor his best officers. He feared an effective commander might become a national hero who would turn against him and be backed by the population. This caused deep bitterness among Diem's generals, some of whom wished to overthrow him.

American advisors became angry that the ARVN was so poorly led. When they complained to their superiors, however, the advisors were

IN THE MEKONG
Ap Bac is in the Mekong Delta's swampy rice paddies. The VC had the advantage of holding dry, wooded ground while the ARVN had to slog in the open through knee-deep muddy water of the paddies.

✱ Battle site

ignored because the U.S. government wanted to hear only good news out of Vietnam. Too much bad news could turn public opinion against American involvement in the conflict. A prime failure of ARVN commanders occurred

GUN IN THE PADDIES
An American military advisor, left, and ARVN soldiers drag a captured 75-mm cannon through a paddy after the Battle of Ap Bac in January 1963. The VC retreated, but the ARVN suffered heavy losses.

Losses	
ARVN:	165 killed/wounded
VC:	12 killed

in the Mekong Delta on January 2, 1963.

ARVN troops, tanks, and helicopters were sent to destroy a small VC base at Ap Bac. U.S. advisor Colonel John Paul Vann oversaw the battle from a plane flying overhead. At a crucial moment, key ARVN commanders ignored Vann's advice and tried to avoid combat. Their inactivity allowed the VC to inflict heavy casualties, killing 80 ARVN and wounding more than 100. Five U.S. helicopters were shot down and three Americans died. Furious, Vann landed and led the final attack that cleared the

NVA OIL CONTAINER
Armies need endless supplies of oil to maintain weapons and machines. This dual-compartment oil can was used by the North Vietnamese Army (NVA) forces operating in the field in South Vietnam.

Military identification mark

village, but most of the VC escaped, taking their dead and wounded.

The resulting critical news reports about Ap Bac upset the Kennedy administration. The United States soon gave secret approval for Vietnamese generals to carry out a military coup against Diem.

THE LEADERSHIP

ALTHOUGH BY 1963 there had been some victories under ARVN leadership, too many South Vietnamese officers were Diem's political appointees. Diem considered that his army's main purpose was to protect his administration from overthrow. Still, ARVN soldiers were brave in battle when well led.

"Cowardice and bumbling [caused] the worst and most humiliating defeat ever inflicted on the Saigon side...."

—Neil Sheehan of the *New York Times*, reporting on Ap Bac

JOHN PAUL VANN (1924-1972)
By openly complaining about ARVN leadership, Vann revealed the tension between U.S. advisors who criticized the ARVN and the high command who excused them. He remained as an ARVN advisor and was killed in a helicopter crash in 1972.

"They chose to reinforce defeat."

—Vann, regarding Diem's unwillingness to spur on his commanders

HUYNH VAN CAO (born 1927)
General Cao, center, confers with American and Vietnamese officers at Hué. As ARVN IV Corps commander in the Mekong Delta, Cao failed to cooperate with Colonel Vann, which resulted in heavy losses for the ARVN troops.

HANOI'S ROAD TO WAR

While fighting the French, the Vietminh had built secret jungle trails to transport supplies and move troops. In 1959, North Vietnam began a new development of military routes into South Vietnam. During the Second Indochina War, this trail system passed through dense jungles that sheltered it from scouting aircraft. Named the Ho Chi Minh Trail in honor of the revolutionary leader, the system grew ever larger and busier.

North Vietnam formed Group 559, a special military unit to oversee construction of these routes, which supported the NVA and Viet Cong fighting in South Vietnam. Commanded by General Vo Bam, Group 559 built trails through the rugged mountains of eastern Laos and Cambodia. This network eventually grew to 12,500 miles (20,000 km) of paths, averaging 22 feet (6.6 m) wide. The trail was maintained by 50,000 troops from the army's engineering corps. In the mid-sixties, up to 50,000 laborers transported supplies along the trail, most carrying backpacks.

BICYCLES ON THE TRAIL
Transport workers on the Ho Chi Minh Trail haul supplies for Viet Cong operations in South Vietnam. Their heavily loaded bicycles have been fitted with specially designed handles for easier steering.

NVA CANTEEN
North Vietnamese soldiers carried little equipment compared to the American and ARVN soldiers with their full backpacks and battle gear. This round NVA water bottle was one of their few essential pieces of field equipment.

Statistics
8,000 men moved along trail monthly (estimated)
20,000 tons of supplies moved along trail monthly (estimated)

Supplies also moved by trucks, bicycles, even elephants. The route was bombed from the air if discovered by the United States, so antiaircraft batteries were stationed along the way to protect it. U.S. bombers could not locate much of the trail, however. There were underground barracks and workshops as well as storage areas for supplies, munitions, and fuel. More than 3,000 miles (5,000 km) of pipeline carried fuel over mountains and under rivers. More than 20,000 tons of supplies moved down the trail each month

WAR ROAD
The Ho Chi Minh Trail was a vast system carrying soldiers and supplies into South Vietnam. The trail was built and operated by North Vietnamese Group 559, which won international fame for its efforts.

HANOI
LAOS
NORTH VIETNAM
CHINA
DMZ
HUÉ
THAILAND
CAMBODIA
PHNOM PENH
SOUTH VIETNAM
Mekong River
SAIGON
SOUTH CHINA SEA

COMMUNIST-HELD AREAS
HO CHI MINH TRAIL
SIHANOUK TRAIL

by 1970. The VC and NVA could not have waged war without the Ho Chi Minh Trail.

THE LEADERSHIP

THE ARCHITECT OF THE Ho Chi Minh Trail was Colonel Dong Si Nguyen, who had the full resources of North Vietnam behind him. After 1964, Nguyen used engineering battalions with the most modern earth-moving and road-building equipment, provided by the Soviets and Chinese.

"Absolute secrecy, absolute secrecy were our watchwords."
—NVA supply commander, interviewed after the war

NORODOM SIHANOUK (born 1922)
Cambodia's Prince Sihanouk tried to stay neutral during the war. The Ho Chi Minh Trail passed through Cambodia, but he dared not block it because that would have angered the North Vietnamese. The southern portion of the trail was nicknamed "Sihanouk Trail."

"Hold them and I'll kill them with airpower. Give me somebody to bomb and I'll win."
—U.S. major general James Hollingsworth, April 1972

PAUL D. HARKINS (1904-1984)
Head of the U.S. MACV until 1964, General Harkins, right, examines a captured enemy rocket launcher. It likely reached South Vietnam on the Ho Chi Minh Trail. Harkins was replaced by General William Westmoreland.

EXCUSE FOR ESCALATION

The South Vietnamese generals launched continual military coups after Diem fell. In 1964, the war effort was faring worse than ever. Fearing a South Vietnamese defeat, President Johnson and the U.S. military looked for opportunities to strike the enemy decisively. Then secret CIA and ARVN operations against Democratic Republic of Vietnam (DRV) sites on the Gulf of Tonkin coast brought on a clash that led to wider war.

ARVN commandos in fast patrol boats had been striking coastal positions, while U.S. naval units were operating not far away. Among these units was the destroyer *Maddox,* which was conducting surveillance patrols in the Gulf of Tonkin. The destroyer was monitoring DRV naval activity near offshore islands and listening to communications. Although in international waters, the *Maddox* was close to a DRV island that had

recently been attacked by commandos. On the afternoon of August 2, three high-speed DRV patrol boats appeared and headed straight for the *Maddox.* Commander Herbert L. Ogier called for air support from the carrier USS *Ticonderoga.* Ogier ordered warning shots, but the patrol boats did not withdraw. Ogier then opened fire, hitting all three boats. The *Maddox* had to avoid torpedoes from the boats, which were then attacked by aircraft from the *Ticonderoga.* The incident was reported to Washington, but President Johnson declined to act rashly in retaliation. He did not order immediate action to punish the North Vietnamese.

Two nights later, on August 4, the *Maddox*'s commander thought he was again under attack. It was dark, with thunderstorms nearby as radar and sonar operators reported 22 enemy torpedoes launched. The *Maddox* and an accompanying destroyer fired into the night. Now Johnson ordered air strikes on North Vietnamese coastal installations. The DRV patrol boat fleet was especially hard hit, with 25 vessels destroyed.

OLD WARHORSE

A World War II-era destroyer that also saw much action in the Korean War, the 376-foot (112 m) *Maddox* was refitted for electronic surveillance operations. She was decommissioned in 1972 and sold to Taiwan, where she was placed in service and renamed *Po Yang.*

Losses	
U.S.:	2 planes shot down
NVA.:	26 patrol boats sunk

On August 7, Congress almost unanimously passed what became known as the Gulf of Tonkin Resolution. This vote gave Johnson broad war powers. He prepared a major air campaign against North Vietnam, and a Marine expeditionary force was readied. The Advisory Phase of the Vietnam conflict was over, and the "Americanization Phase" had begun. Years later, it was found there had been no second DRV attack in the Gulf of Tonkin.

✳ PRESUMED ATTACKS ON U.S. WARSHIPS

NAVAL CLASH
The destroyer USS *Maddox* engaged DRV patrol boats in the Gulf of Tonkin on August 2, 1965. Farther south two days later, a second engagement was reported. These incidents led Congress to authorize a widening of the Vietnam conflict.

THE LEADERSHIP

OGIER HAD COMMANDED THE *Maddox* since 1962. His destroyer was part of "Desoto Patrol," supporting CIA-led coastal raids. Also aboard the *Maddox* was Ogier's superior, Captain John J. Herrick, commander of Destroyer Division 192. Ogier resigned a few days after the Tonkin incident.

"North Vietnamese vessels chased away the U.S. pirates…on the sea and in the air."
—Radio Hanoi news announcement, August 1964

PHAM VAN DONG (1908-2000)
DRV prime minister between 1950 and 1976, Dong was from a wealthy family. With Ho Chi Minh, he founded the Indochinese Communist Party in 1930. Dong and General Giap were co-chairmen of the DRV National Defense Council during the Second Indochina War.

"[Like] Grandma's nightshirt — it covered everything."
Johnson, on Gulf of Tonkin Resolution war powers

LYNDON B. JOHNSON (1908-1973)
LBJ most of all wanted his presidency to develop social policy that helped the poor. Yet he feared "losing" Vietnam to Communist expansion. This caused him to escalate U.S. involvement in Vietnam. He is shown signing the Gulf of Tonkin Resolution.

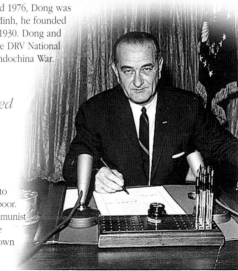

America Hopes for Quick Victory

The Gulf of Tonkin Resolution gave President Johnson the authority to use American military might against North Vietnam and the Viet Cong. The "Advisory Phase" of the Vietnam War was over.

Johnson believed the conflict could be won quickly with well-trained U.S. troops supported by the most advanced weaponry and technology. He hoped American air power would force North Vietnam to halt its aggression against the South.

The Operation Rolling Thunder bombing campaign against North Vietnam began on March 2, 1965. Next, marines waded ashore on March 8 to defend an airfield at Da Nang, South Vietnam. Across America, television screens showed the marines jumping down from amphibious landing craft. Americans hoped for a speedy victory and an early return home for their troops. The Da Nang

HELICOPTER ASSAULT
Paratroopers of the 173rd Airborne Brigade assemble for action near Saigon in 1965. They have just been landed by the helicopters that hover overhead in close support.

March	April	May	July
Rolling Thunder air campaign begins	President Johnson authorizes Westmoreland to go on the offensive	Johnson announces first pause in the bombing campaign	50,000 more troops sent to Vietnam
Marines land at Da Nang			U.S. Coastal Surveillance Force formed
Market Time begins			

deployment was followed by 23,000 more troops in June and 50,000 in July. By the end of 1965 there would be 184,300 troops in Vietnam.

By August, it seemed the war might be won quickly. A Marine offensive, Operation Starlite, destroyed a large VC force. In November, U.S. Army units used helicopters for the first time to ride into battle and smash two NVA regiments in the Ia Drang Valley.

Yet, the NVA and VC could take heavy casualties and fight on. Ho Chi Minh had warned the French in the First Indochina War: "You can kill ten of my men for every one I kill of yours, but even at those odds, you will lose and I will win."

As the Second Indochina War began, most U.S. leaders failed to fully learn from the lessons of the first war.

NEWS COVERAGE

As American involvement in Vietnam deepened, U.S. television showed events firsthand: Buddhist riots, marines landing, warplanes in action. For the first time, television brought images of an ongoing war directly into the American home. Yet reporters did not explain the war's origins, so Americans did not understand what the conflict was about. Few knew anything of Vietnam's long struggle for independence.

UNDER FIRE
Courageous photographers risked their lives to photograph front-line combat. This photographer is with airborne troops.

WAIST-DEEP IN WATER
Marines wade through surf after leaving their landing craft during Operation Piranha in September 1965. This was a search-and-destroy mission to shut down a VC infiltration and supply network along the coast.

August	October	November	December
Operation Starlite is first major U.S. offensive	NVA attacks U.S. Special Forces camp at Plei Me in Central Highlands	Battle of Ia Drang Valley LZ X-Ray LZ Albany	U.S. troop levels reach 184,300 Johnson pauses Rolling Thunder a second time

STRATEGIC BOMBING

Just hours after the Gulf of Tonkin incident, U.S. carrier-based fighter-bombers hit North Vietnam. This strike began a bombing campaign that opened a new conflict, which Americans soon would call the Vietnam War. The air campaign began on March 2, 1965, and was given the code name Operation Rolling Thunder. This operation continued until 1968.

At first, air attacks were aimed at southern areas of North Vietnam, near the Ho Chi Minh Trail. U.S. military planners wanted to stop supplies flowing down the trail to the VC in South Vietnam. In 1966, U.S. and ARVN planes also attacked oil storage sites and ammunition dumps in North Vietnam. They were met with heavy antiaircraft fire, surface-to-air missiles, and North Vietnam Air Force fighter

planes. President Johnson further widened the bombings in 1967 and 1968. He ordered attacks on factories, power plants, and airfields around Hanoi and the important port of Haiphong. Johnson gradually increased the intensity of the bombing as the war went on.

During Rolling Thunder 643,000 tons of bombs were dropped on North Vietnam—more than were dropped on Japan during World War II. Though the bombing caused great destruction, the NVA war effort continued in full force, and military supplies poured south to the VC.

Rolling Thunder also had political goals. Johnson and Defense Secretary Robert S. McNamara thought Ho Chi Minh would agree to peace talks in order to stop the air campaign. Seven

HEADING NORTH TO STRIKE
U.S. Air Force Thunderchiefs are refueled on their way to bomb North Vietnam during Operation Rolling Thunder in January 1966. They hook up to a KC-135 Stratotanker—its tail at right. By refueling in the air, bombers could fly from distant bases to attack North Vietnam.

Statistics 1965–1968

922 aircraft lost
304,000 fighter-bomber sorties
2,380 B-52 bomber sorties
643,000 tons of bombs dropped

times, Johnson ordered a halt to air strikes to show that the United States was willing to negotiate. The North Vietnamese were not brought to the negotiating table, however. Instead, they used the bombing halts to rebuild factories and roads that had been destroyed.

By 1968, it was clear the political and military goals of Rolling Thunder had failed. Johnson ordered an end to the bombing campaign on October 31, 1968.

BOMBING ROUTES
The heaviest bombardments of North Vietnam came from B-52 bombers based in Guam and Okinawa. U.S. fighter-bombers flew bombing missions from air bases in South Vietnam and Thailand, and from carriers in the Gulf of Tonkin.

■■■ B-52 ROUTES FROM OKINAWA AND GUAM

THE LEADERSHIP

PRESIDENT JOHNSON AND HIS ADVISORS chose the Rolling Thunder targets, avoiding heavy bombing near cities. Air Force generals disagreed with such restrictions. They wanted to hit harder and widen the choice of targets.

AMERICAN PILOT
Commander George Jacobssen Jr., gives the okay sign aboard carrier USS *Ranger* after returning from a Rolling Thunder mission in 1965. Jacobssen led strikes on an NVA ammunition dump. U.S. pilots were attacked by North Vietnamese fighter pilots flying Russian-made MiGs and were fired on by surface-to-air missiles.

"Senior airmen pressed for the extension of Rolling Thunder into an air strategy focused upon the heart of North Vietnam."
—General William Momyer, USAF

HO CHI MINH (1890-1969)
President Ho Chi Minh talks to the crew of an antiaircraft gun in December 1966. Ho said that every North Vietnamese had a role in the national defense. Civilians worked rebuilding roads and bridges damaged by the bombings.

"The bombs heightened rather than dampened our spirit."
—North Vietnam's Ton That Tung

A FIRST VICTORY

Viet Cong guerrillas attacked throughout South Vietnam in early 1965. They hit ARVN bases and ambushed troop columns. The attacks soon became more daring, threatening U.S. air bases used in Operation Rolling Thunder. General William Westmoreland, commander of MACV (Military Assistance Command, Vietnam), called for U.S. forces to secure the airfields.

President Johnson was faced with a hard decision: whether or not to send in combat troops. Johnson and his advisors decided ARVN forces were too weak to resist the VC. American troops were needed. On March 8, 1965, 4,000 marines began coming ashore to protect the air base at Da Nang. This was the first major deployment of U.S. ground troops in South Vietnam. They were soon followed by thousands more American troops. Plans were underway for 125,000 troops to deploy in Vietnam.

As VC attacks increased, Johnson gave permission for Westmoreland to go on the offensive. Now U.S. troops would be doing more than defending bases and advising ARVN forces. The first offensive was Operation Starlite. In August, U.S. general Lewis W. Walt learned a VC force of 1,500 men was planning to attack the Chu Lai airfield. General Walt decided to strike first. He chose August 18 for Operation Starlite.

SEARCH AND DESTROY
Marines guard VC fighters captured in Operation Starlite. The prisoners wait to be transported out of the combat area south of Chu Lai by Marine Corps helicopters.

Losses	
U.S.:	45 killed, 120 wounded
VC:	614 killed, 9 taken prisoner

More than 5,500 marines surprised the VC, camped near the coast 12 miles (19 km) from Chu Lai. Marines came ashore in an amphibious assault as others were carried into battle by helicopter. The VC stubbornly defended fortified hamlets and hills, giving the marines a bitter fight. The marines were backed by superior U.S. firepower. At least 3,000 artillery rounds were fired by American guns at Chu Lai, with 290 supporting attacks by fighter-bombers. Warships off shore fired 1,562 rounds at the enemy.

The battle continued until August 24, when Operation Starlite was

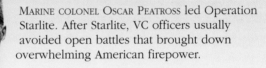

COASTAL BASE
Most American bases were along the coast of South Vietnam, where they could be easily supplied and defended by U.S. warships. Operation Starlite was fought to secure an air base south of the South Vietnamese city of Hué.

✳ BATTLE SITE

completed, and the strength of the VC regiment had been broken. The Marines lost 45 killed and 120 wounded to 614 VC killed. U.S. troops had won a major victory in their first operation.

THE LEADERSHIP

MARINE COLONEL OSCAR PEATROSS led Operation Starlite. After Starlite, VC officers usually avoided open battles that brought down overwhelming American firepower.

"How many years the war goes on depends on you and not us."

—DRV President Pham Van Dong, statement to the United States

NGUYEN HUU THO (1910–1996)
A French-educated lawyer, Tho became chairman of the National Liberation Front (NLF), the organization that controlled the VC. Tho was jailed by the French during the First Indochina War, and later by Ngo Dinh Diem's regime. After escaping from prison, Tho led the VC against U.S. and ARVN forces. He became vice president of Vietnam after the war.

"I extend my heartfelt thanks to the military units which have achieved clear-cut victory against the last Viet Cong regiment of Chu Lai."

—President Johnson to marines who fought in Starlite

WILLIAM C. WESTMORELAND (born 1914)
A West Pointer and veteran of World War II and the Korean War, General Westmoreland took command of MACV in 1964. When U.S. combat troops landed in 1965, Westmoreland was the highest-ranking officer in Vietnam. He led U.S. forces there until replaced in 1968.

SWIFT BOATS AND CUTTERS

Before 1965, military supplies to the Viet Cong were mostly smuggled by sea from North Vietnam to ports in the South. Sailing ships, called "junks," and oar-powered "sampans" slipped past ARVN naval patrols. The poorly trained South Vietnamese Navy could not slow this flood of arms and military equipment.

On March 11, 1965, General Westmoreland put Operation Market Time into action to stop the arms flow. Headquartered at Cam Ranh Bay, the Coastal Surveillance Force patrolled the 1,200-mile (1,931-km) coastline of South Vietnam. Market Time used naval destroyers, Coast Guard cutters, and smaller "Swift" boats. The 55-foot (17-m) Swifts operated close to shore. Armed with machine guns and mortars, these speedy boats could intercept suspicious vessels. The cutters and destroyers patrolled farther out to sea. Long-range patrol planes flew up and down the coast and over the sea.

While Americans heard news of battles in Vietnam, little was known about these sailors' dangerous jobs. During the height of the war, from 1966 through 1967, the Coastal Surveillance Force searched more than 700,000 Vietnamese junks, sampans, and other vessels. From 1965 to 1971, it succeeded in completely closing sea routes to South Vietnam.

TWENTY DONG
The dong was the currency of the South Vietnamese government. Cash bribes paid to corrupt ARVN officers allowed some supplies to get through to the VC.

PATROLLING VIETNAM'S WATERS
American sailors aboard the minesweeper USS *Loyalty* pull alongside a Vietnamese fishing boat to search it.

Statistics

During Market Time a Vietnamese vessel was inspected every 15–20 seconds

With sea traffic stopped, the VC received supplies coming down the Ho Chi Minh Trail and through the neutral Cambodian port of Sihanoukville. In 1969, Sihanoukville was closed to Communist shipping and the Ho Chi Minh Trail became the only supply route.

When U.S. forces began to pull out of Vietnam in 1970, the Swift boats and Coast Guard cutters were turned over to the South Vietnamese Navy, which took over Market Time operations from 1971 to 1975.

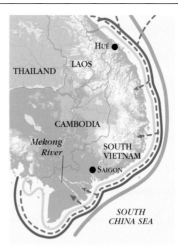

NAVAL BLOCKADE
Market Time established three "interdiction zones" to interdict, or cut, the enemy's line of supply by water. Farthest out to sea was the air interdiction zone, closer in was the sea force zone, and closest was the coastal zone.

▬▬▬ SEA FORCE INTERDICTION ZONE
▬▬▬ AIR INTERDICTION ZONE
▬▬▬ COASTAL ZONE AND MARKET TIME BOUNDARY
■ ■ ■ NVA SEA INFILTRATION ROUTES

THE LEADERSHIP

FROM 1966 ON, MARKET TIME operations were led by Naval Forces, Vietnam, headquartered in Saigon. Admiral Elmo R. Zumwalt Jr. headed this command from 1968 to 1970.

MADAME NGUYEN THI BINH (born 1927)
Binh was a high-ranking official in the NLF during hostilities with the U.S. She was chief representative of the NLF during the 1973 Paris Peace Talks and later vice president of Vietnam. One third of the top NLF political officers were women.

"American policy destroyed our nation and caused the separation of our people."
—Madame Nguyen Thi Binh

ULYSSES S.G. SHARP (1906–2001)
A graduate of the U.S. Naval Academy, Admiral Sharp was commander in chief of the Pacific Command from 1964 to 1968. Based in Honolulu, Sharp was responsible for military strategy throughout the Pacific, including Vietnam.

"Market Time forces ... have successfully blocked intrusions via the sea, forcing the enemy to use the long, tortuous Ho Chi Minh trail."
—Westmoreland, November 1968

AIRMOBILE WARFARE

The Battle of the Ia Drang Valley was a series of engagements between the North Vietnamese Army and the U.S. Army's First Cavalry Division. U.S. troops had fought VC guerrillas in Operation Starlite, but had yet to meet the NVA. Then, in the fall of 1965, "First Cav" collided with veteran NVA forces in the Ia Drang Valley of South Vietnam's Central Highlands. This was the first major engagement between American forces and well-trained and equipped NVA troops.

A JUNGLE CLEARING
U.S. First Cavalry troopers spread out and cautiously advance across open ground in the mountainous jungle of An Khe Pass during the Battle of the Ia Drang in October 1965.

Through 1964 and 1965, North Vietnamese leadership had been preparing a campaign to split the South in two. Tens of thousands of troops journeyed down the Ho Chi Minh Trail to assemble across the border in Cambodia. This force was to drive through the Central Highlands and down to the sea. On October 19, 1965, the offensive began with an attack on the U.S. Special Forces base at Plei Me. NVA regiments surrounded the base, which was garrisoned by a 12-man Special Forces team and 350 fighters from the local Montagnard people. NVA ambushes were prepared along the road to the city of Pleiku,

Losses	
U.S.:	1,000 killed/wounded/missing
NVA:	6,000 killed (estimated)

40 miles (64 km) to the north. The NVA planned to surprise and destroy any reinforcements sent from Pleiku to rescue Plei Me.

The American response was a new kind of "airmobile" warfare. The First Air Cavalry Division rode into combat by helicopters that flew past NVA ambushes to land directly on the battlefield. On October 26, ARVN ground units supported by the airmobile division broke through to Plei Mei. NVA forces retreated southwest toward the Ia Drang Valley.

Now Westmoreland sent the First Air Cavalry on the offensive. They were to helicopter southward to find and destroy retreating NVA regiments. The

IA DRANG
Following an NVA attack on a Special Forces camp at Plei Me in October 1965, U.S. and ARVN troops counterattacked by helicopter.

▬▬▬	NVA ATTACKS
▪▪▪▪	NVA RETREATS
▬▬▬	U.S. AND ARVN AIR ATTACKS

Americans did not know that the NVA commander, General Chu Huy Man, had been reinforced by 2,000 fresh troops. At a well-supplied base in the Ia Drang Valley, Man rested his forces, preparing for another attack on Plei Me.

THE LEADERSHIP

ARMY GENERAL HAMILTON HOWZE developed the new airmobile tactics. Ia Drang saw the first direct support of ground combat by B-52 heavy bombers of the Seventh Air Force. All U.S. Southeast Asia forces were led by Admiral Ulysses S. Sharp, commander in chief, Pacific, 1964–1968.

CHU HUY MAN (born 1920)
General Man was the first NVA commander to lead a large force into battle against major American units. Defeated at the Ia Drang, he soon regrouped to attack new positions established by American airmobile troops.

"[My goal was] to draw the Americans into battle to learn how they fight and teach my men how to kill them."
—General Man, after the war

"My battalion had come looking for trouble in the Ia Drang; we had found all we wanted and more."
—Colonel Harold G. Moore, First Battalion, Seventh Cavalry Regiment

HARRY W.O. KINNARD (born 1915)
General Kinnard, right, meets with Secretary of Defense McNamara at the An Khe base of the First Cavalry Division, which Kinnard commanded at Ia Drang. McNamara toured the battlefield in November 1969.

AIR CAVALRY OFFENSIVE

U.S. headquarters thought NVA troops retreating from their failed siege of Plei Me were scattered in defeat. General Harry Kinnard, commander of the First Cavalry Division, did not know the NVA had regrouped—or that they had received 2,000 reinforcements. Kinnard began to search for enemy forces in November. His strategy was to defeat them by sending in large numbers of "heliborne" troops and using overwhelming firepower.

On November 14, U.S. air cavalry forces flew into what seemed an undefended landing zone (LZ), named X-Ray, in the Ia Drang Valley. These 430 troops of the Seventh Air Cavalry Regiment were under Lieutenant Colonel Harold G. Moore. Their mission was to conduct patrols in nearby mountains, searching for enemy bases. Within a few hours, the air cavalry were surrounded and under attack from 2,000 NVA. General Chu Huy Man saw a chance to destroy the Americans and ordered an all-out assault. The struggle was savagely fought. Determined NVA attacks almost overran the U.S. positions, but Moore and his men held on. At times they were locked in hand-to-hand fighting with the enemy.

U.S. reinforcements flew in by helicopter, and intense artillery and air strikes helped stop the NVA attacks. On the morning of November 15, additional U.S. reinforcements arrived. That same day, devastating strikes by B-52s and fighter-bombers forced the NVA

Losses LZ X-Ray and LZ Albany	
U.S.:	234 killed, 245 wounded
NVA:	2,403 killed

PREPARING FOR BATTLE
Troopers of the airmobile First Cavalry Division get ready to board arriving assault helicopters on October 25, 1965, during the Ia Drang campaign.

to retreat. U.S. dead numbered 79, with 121 wounded, while NVA casualties were estimated at more than 2,000.

The victory at LZ X-Ray was soon followed by another bitter fight nearby, when 400 air cavalry moving overland were ambushed. On November 17, fresh NVA troops attacked this American column at a jungle clearing called LZ Albany. In a fierce all-day battle, 155 U.S. troops were killed and 124 wounded. NVA dead numbered 403, with 150 wounded. Reinforcements and massive air strikes saved the U.S. survivors, who were airlifted out on November 20.

DUC CO
■ SPECIAL FORCES CAMP

SOUTH VIETNAM

Route 19

LZ ALBANY

LZ COLUMBUS
LZ FALCON

LZ X-RAY
Chu Pong Mtn.

■ PLEI ME SPECIAL FORCES CAMP

LZ VICTOR

✳ AMBUSH
■ U.S. LANDING ZONES
▬ NVA ATTACKS
■ ■ ■ ■ NVA RETREATS

COUNTERSTRIKE NVA forces that had been driven from positions threatening the Special Forces camp at Plei Me were replaced by fresh units. These regiments surprised heliborne First Cavalry troops at landing zones X-Ray and Albany.

For U.S. commanders, LZ X-Ray proved the effectiveness of transporting infantry into battle by helicopter. The defeat at Albany, however, showed that veteran NVA troops were ready to fight again after taking terrible losses.

THE LEADERSHIP

MACV COMMANDER WESTMORELAND was enthusiastic about the number of enemy casualties inflicted in the Ia Drang fighting. His airmobile tactics and search-and-destroy strategy were succeeding. NVA general Man was defeated in his plan to march to the coast and split South Vietnam in two.

NGUYEN HUU AN (born 1920)
Colonel An was NVA battlefield commander at LZ Albany. An considered the engagement an NVA victory. At LZ Albany, he called for tactics to get close to the Americans—"grab them by the belt"—so U.S. air power and artillery would be unable to strike.

"It raised our soldiers' morale and gave us many good lessons."
—Colonel An, discussing the fight at LZ Albany

HAROLD G. MOORE (born 1922)
Colonel Moore was a West Point graduate, a master parachutist, and an Army aviator. He commanded two infantry companies in the Korean War. After leading the First Battalion, Seventh Cavalry, in Vietnam, he rose to the rank of general. Moore co-authored a book about Ia Drang: *We Were Soldiers Once…and Young.*

"[LZ Albany] was the most savage one-day battle of the Vietnam War."
—Moore and co-author Joseph Galloway

Building Bases, Winning Trust

Before the U.S. military came to South Vietnam, Saigon was the only major port. By 1966, six new harbors had been built, including a massive naval base at Cam Ranh Bay.

American engineers built huge new military bases in just a few months. Helicopters, bombers, fighters, and transport planes made South Vietnam's airports the busiest in the world. With the arrival of U.S. and allied troops, such as the Australians, dollars poured into the country. Saigon changed quickly from a quiet town to a great and bustling metropolis.

President Johnson wanted his troops to win the "hearts and minds"— the trust and friendship—of the Vietnamese. Villages destroyed by fighting were rebuilt, and medical officers supplied vaccines and medicines. Yet, as soon as Americans

BLINDFOLDED PRISONER
A trooper of the U.S. First Cavalry Division leads a suspected Viet Cong prisoner during Operation Irving in October 1966. This campaign was one of several that assaulted VC strongholds in central South Vietnam's Binh Dinh Province.

January	March	April	May
Operation White Wing begins	Attempt to repeal Gulf of Tonkin Resolution is defeated in Congress	First Australian Task Force (ATF) is formed	Marines attacked by NVA at Dong Ha
	Operation White Wing ends		

left a village, VC officers returned to ruthlessly punish anyone who had aided their enemy. U.S. troops were in constant danger. Every villager might be a VC guerrilla hiding a hand grenade or machine gun.

As bases were completed in 1966, offensives were launched to clear out the VC. Operation White Wing lasted from January to March, and in August the Australians won the Battle of Long Tan. In September, Operation Attleboro cleared the region northwest of Saigon as VC forces retreated across the borders into Cambodia and Laos. U.S. troops could not follow into these neutral countries, however, and the VC soon returned to South Vietnam.

By the end of 1966, there were 389,000 U.S. troops in Vietnam.

ROCKETS FLASH
A U.S. Navy Phantom F4B from the carrier USS *Enterprise* fires rockets at Viet Cong positions in September 1966. Rockets are carried under the fighter's wings.

DEADLY AGENT

Operation Ranch Hand, 1962–1970, was a U.S. campaign to destroy forests that gave cover to VC and NVA forces. Without trees and bushes to hide behind, it was harder for guerrillas to ambush U.S. and ARVN troops or to move supplies. Aircraft sprayed the jungle with almost 19 million gallons of herbicides—chemicals that kill vegetation. The most commonly used herbicide was "Agent Orange." Many U.S. veterans and Vietnamese developed severe health problems, which are thought to have been caused by exposure to dioxin, a chemical used in herbicides.

OPERATION RANCH HAND
U.S. Air Force C-123s spray a 1,000 foot-(300 m-) wide path of "defoliating liquid" (herbicide) to destroy VC jungle cover.

August	September	November	December
Australians win the Battle of Long Tan	Operation Attleboro begins	Operation Attleboro ends; huge VC weapons cache discovered	U.S. troop levels reach 389,000
	Nguyen Van Thieu elected president of South Vietnam		

FREE WORLD FORCES

Free World Military Assistance Forces in South Vietnam included combat troops from Australia, Thailand, New Zealand, the Philippines, and South

> *"Your troops have won one of the most spectacular [victories] in Vietnam to date."*
> —Westmoreland to Australians who fought at Long Tan

Korea. The Australian Task Force (ATF) quickly won fame for skill in jungle fighting. The ATF controlled a region 35 miles (56 km) southeast of Saigon.

AMBUSH!
The ATF was based at Nui Dat, an area of high ground surrounded by jungle and rubber plantations. At nearby Long Tan, a large VC force ambushed an ATF patrol.

✳ BATTLE SITE

On August 18, a 101-man ATF force was ambushed by 2,500 VC near the Long Tan rubber plantation. The Australians beat off all attacks until reinforced. In recognition of their bravery, the Australian government made August 18 "Vietnam Veterans Day." Australian forces were withdrawn from Vietnam in 1971.

THE LEADERSHIP

AUSTRALIAN OFFICERS FAVORED DEADLY marksmanship and jungle ambushes to fight the VC. The U.S. strategy was to win with rapid concentration of forces and overwhelming firepower.

O.D. JACKSON
General Jackson was the first commander of Australian troops in Vietnam. In April 1966, he took charge of the ATF (Australian Task Force) and began "aggressive patrolling." This meant driving a wedge between enemy forces and the villages.

AUSSIES ON PATROL
Australian soldiers cautiously wade through mangrove swamps while on patrol near the Saigon River in 1966. "Aussies" favored soft jungle hats instead of heavy steel helmets.

Losses

Australians:	18 killed, 24 wounded
VC:	245 killed, 500 wounded, 3 taken prisoner

VIET CONG BASE DISCOVERED

The 196th Light Infantry Brigade began Operation Attleboro on September 14 with a sweep northwest of Saigon. The operation went quietly until November 3, when troops led by Major Guy S. Meloy made contact with the VC. A three-day battle began as the VC fought fiercely to defend an enormous base camp and weapons cache. Outnumbered, Meloy was reinforced until he had almost the entire brigade under his command. He held out, and by November 15 the VC were defeated. Of the 1,106 VC dead, many were officers, who were difficult to replace.

"He looked at me as if to say, 'Thanks for trying,' and died."

—Meloy, on a wounded soldier who has watched his evacuation helicopter crash

NEAR SAIGON
Operation Attleboro uncovered an enormous weapons cache at a base northwest of Saigon. This was near a VC area that Americans termed the "Iron Triangle" because it was so strongly defended.

✹ BATTLE SITE

THE LEADERSHIP

IN ATTLEBORO, VC LEADERS suffered heavy casualties. Westmoreland hoped that attacking VC bases would bring the guerrillas to battle. Colonel Jack Whitted's First Battalion, Twenty-eighth Infantry Regiment, helped capture the main VC weapons cache, including 19,000 grenades.

GUY S. MELOY (born 1930)
Though wounded, Major Meloy, left, continues to direct the First Battalion, Twenty-seventh Infantry Regiment. While lieutenant colonels normally led battalions, Meloy was given command because of his outstanding ability. He later became a general commanding the Eighty-second Airborne Division.

INTO THE DEPTHS
A soldier of the 196th Light Infantry Brigade explores a 40 foot– (12 m–) deep VC well during operation Attleboro in October 1966.

Losses	
U.S.:	155 killed, 494 wounded
VC/NVA:	1,106 killed

45

U.S. Casualties Mount, Bombing Intensifies

Through 1967, Westmoreland followed a strategy of "attrition." This meant causing as many casualties as possible on the VC and NVA. He expected superior U.S. firepower to defeat the Communists.

U.S. and ARVN troops carried out large "search-and-destroy" missions that struck at enemy base areas. In January, Operation Cedar Falls sent troops into the "Iron Triangle." This was a VC stronghold of dense forest and wet rice lands near Saigon. Operation Junction City soon followed, attacking north of the capital. The VC suffered heavy losses and had to retreat, but they returned after the Americans moved out.

Aggressively bringing on action cost Westmoreland's forces heavily. In 1967, American deaths in Vietnam totaled 9,378, compared with 5,008 in 1966 and 1,369 in 1965.

In order to stop military aid from reaching North Vietnam, U.S. air power attacked roads and bridges to China.

PREPARING TO ASSAULT
Members of the 173rd Airborne Brigade are briefed just before their attack on Hill 875 in November 1967. This fortified hill, southwest of Dak To, was taken on Thanksgiving Day after fierce fighting.

January	February	April	May
Operation Bolo Operation Cedar Falls	Operation Junction City	Civilian casualties bring about antiwar demonstrations in New York and San Francisco	Operation Junction City ends; NVA/VC base with huge arms cache is found

In air combat, Operation Bolo destroyed seven of North Vietnam's 16 MiG fighters. Continued heavy bombing damaged the North's industrial and transport capability, but bombing campaigns stirred up opposition in the United States. News of civilian casualties led to huge antiwar protests.

At the end of the year, the NVA brought on the Battle of Dak To near the Laotian border. Such "border battles" drew U.S. troops away from the cities, where the VC were planning an uprising. Military intelligence knew a major enemy effort was coming but did not know how or when.

By the end of 1967, more than 485,000 U.S. military personnel were "in country," as soldiers termed their tour of duty in Vietnam. That number would continue to rise.

SEARCHING FOR THE ENEMY
M-113 armored personnel carriers transport soldiers of the Twenty-fifth Infantry Division near the Saigon River during Operation Cedar Falls. This search-and-destroy mission rooted out NVA and VC fighters north of Saigon.

ANTIWAR MOVEMENT

Most Americans at first supported military involvement in Vietnam, but opposition was developing by 1963. Many colleges and high schools held "teach-ins" to discuss and study the conflict. There was much open debate in public forums, and antiwar protests began to be held. In 1965, demonstrations took place in New York and Washington, D.C. As more American soldiers died and no end to the war seemed in sight, opposition steadily increased. By 1969, antiwar marchers on Washington numbered in the hundreds of thousands. These demonstrations continued to grow.

CONFRONTATION
Military police guard Department of Defense headquarters at the Pentagon as antiwar protesters sit down during the October 1967 march on Washington, D.C. At least 70,000 people gathered to oppose the war.

July	October	November	December
Giap begins plans for a major NVA offensive in South Vietnamese cities	Giap attacks U.S. Special Forces camps to draw troops out of the cities	At least 70,000 peace protesters march on the Pentagon	Battle of Dak To ends
			485,000 U.S. troops in Vietnam

PHANTOMS SPRING A TRAP

President Johnson intended the "Rolling Thunder" bombing to force the North Vietnamese to ask for peace. The campaign was tightly controlled, however, and did not use high-flying heavy bombers. Johnson did not want to be accused of ruthlessly killing North Vietnamese civilians. Most missions were carried out by almost-obsolete F-105 fighter-bombers. Further, American pilots could not bomb Hanoi and Haiphong. Nor were they allowed to strike North Vietnamese Air Force (NVAF) planes on the ground near these cities. The only enemy planes that could be attacked were those in the air.

By the close of 1966, 455 U.S. warplanes had been shot down. NVA antiaircraft weaponry provided by the Soviets was improving, as was the

NVAF, which acquired 16 new MiG-21s. These Soviet-made "interceptors" flew at 1,385 mph (2,200 kmph) and were armed with air-to-air missiles. Their high-speed attacks had shot down 10 bombers and forced many others to break off missions early.

Colonel Robin Olds, commander of the U.S. Eighth Tactical Fighter Wing, planned to draw the MiG-21s into action against his F-4 Phantom fighters, which were superior to the F-105s.

On January 2, 1967, 56 F-4 fighters flew toward Hanoi in a mission code-named "Bolo." Olds had his planes fly with the same formation, speed, and altitude as F-105 bombers. They also used the same radar-jamming equipment and radio call-signs. To NVA air defenses, the F-4s seemed like F-105s. The trap worked, and the MiG-21s rose to the attack. By this time, however, there were only 12 F-4s. The rest had run into bad

ON A MISSION

Two U.S. Air Force Phantom fighters patrol the skies over Southeast Asia in January 1967. MiGs shot down 42 F-4C Phantoms over Vietnam, 22 of them with heat-seeking missiles. In 1972, Phantoms carried the first laser-guided "smart" bombs for precision strikes.

Losses Operation Bolo	
U.S.:	none
NVA:	7 MiG fighters destroyed

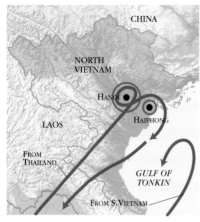

BOLO MISSION
U.S. F-4 Phantoms from bases in Thailand and South Vietnam destroyed many of the NVAF's best fighters on January 2, 1967. U.S. planes were not permitted to strike main cities or near the Chinese border.

weather and turned back. The F-4 Phantoms engaged the enemy in a 15-minute dogfight, shooting down seven MiGs without American loss.

LBJ temporarily halted the bombing in February, but Hanoi did not respond. Rolling Thunder resumed in March, now targeting industrial sites and power plants in cities. By the end of 1967, 649 American aircraft had been lost, and the wider bombing had stirred up harsh criticism internationally and at home.

THE LEADERSHIP

JOHNSON AND DEFENSE SECRETARY McNamara limited bombing targets. Soviet military technicians taught the NVA how to use surface-to-air missile systems, 95 of which were provided by the Soviet Union.

"If the enemy attacks us from above, we will attack him from below."

—Truong Chinh, North Vietnamese Communist theorist

NVAF PILOTS
These Soviet-trained MiG pilots discuss air-combat tactics at their base in North Vietnam in 1967. MiGs shot down 137 U.S. aircraft, with two types of MiGs accounting for 129 of them: MiG-21s had 68 victories, and MiG-17s had 61.

"[The U.S. bombing] campaign demonstrated not strength and determination but political weakness and uncertainty."

—Westmoreland, complaining years later about bombing policy

WING COMMANDER
Colonel Robin Olds prepares to climb aboard his F-4 Phantom at a Southeast Asia base in 1967. In Operation Bolo, Olds accounted for one of seven MiG-21s shot down in a brief but deadly dogfight near Hanoi.

CRACKING THE IRON TRIANGLE

The Iron Triangle was a fortified VC base area just 35 miles (56 km) northwest of Saigon. This was a huge complex of tunnels and defensive works. From here, the VC launched

> *"I've always said,
> if you don't go in to win,
> don't go in at all."*
>
> —Haig, objecting to U.S. military strategy

STRONGHOLD
Cedar Falls destroyed 525 VC tunnels in the Iron Triangle, an area of 116 square miles (300 sq. km) on the Saigon River.

missions against Saigon and then returned to safety. In Operation Cedar Falls, U.S. and ARVN infantry, paratroops, armor, and heliborne air cavalry pushed deep into the Iron Triangle. U.S. commanders hoped the VC would fight to defend their bases, as they had during Operation Attleboro, where they took heavy casualties. In Cedar Falls, most VC fled as the offensive destroyed tunnels and burned down villages sympathetic to the VC.

THE LEADERSHIP

THE IRON TRIANGLE HELD A VC military region headquarters. When attacked, the VC officer staff fled, leaving behind documents, maps, and plans. Two days after Cedar Falls ended, the VC began returning.

ALEXANDER HAIG (born 1924)
Colonel Haig led a battalion of the Twenty-sixth Infantry Division in Cedar Falls. He rose to general, was liaison between the Pentagon and White House, became NATO supreme commander, and in 1981 was named U.S. secretary of state.

BOOBY TRAP
A U.S. Army engineer carefully examines a booby trap set on a forest path during Cedar Falls in January 1967. The path leads to a VC tunnel in the Iron Triangle.

Losses	
U.S.:	72 killed, 337 wounded
VC:	750 killed, 280 prisoners
ARVN:	3 killed, 8 wounded

THE LARGEST OFFENSIVE

This operation aimed to wipe out VC leaders of the Central Office for South Vietnam (COSVN). The target area, along the Cambodian border, was labeled War Zone C. Junction City involved 22 U.S. infantry and 14 artillery battalions, and four ARVN battalions. It was the largest search-and-destroy mission of the war and included the first major combat parachute assault since the Korean War. The VC launched a series of counterattacks against Junction City forces in March and April. Each time the VC were beaten off with heavy losses. By May, Junction City had badly mauled a VC division but had not discovered COSVN headquarters.

"[General Westmoreland] said, in effect, 'Think big.'"

—General Seaman, describing the U.S. high command's orders

LAOS
CAMBODIA
SOUTH VIETNAM
AIR ASSAULTS
Mekong River
GROUND ASSAULTS
SAIGON
SOUTH CHINA SEA

JUNCTION CITY OPERATIONAL AREA
U.S. ATTACKS

JUNCTION CITY
War Zone C, north of Saigon, was fertile agricultural country crisscrossed by rivers. In the air assault, U.S. forces flew over neutral Cambodian territory, which was illegal.

THE LEADERSHIP

JUNCTION CITY AND CEDAR FALLS were the first large-scale operations involving U.S. and South Vietnamese forces. The highest VC leaders had used this remote region as a stronghold and sanctuary for 20 years.

Insignia of the First Infantry Division

JONATHAN O. SEAMAN (1911–1986)
General Seaman commanded the U.S. First Infantry Division, a main unit in Junction City. Also, he had led the larger organization, II Field Force, Vietnam, since early 1966. Seaman oversaw both the Cedar Falls and Junction City operations.

MOBILE ARTILLERY
Gunners of the U.S. Thirty-second Artillery Regiment prepare to fire a 175-mm cannon at VC positions during Junction City. The gun is mounted on tracks that give it mobility.

Losses	
U.S.:	282 killed, 1,576 wounded
VC:	2,728 killed, 34 taken prisoner

COURAGE AND AIR STRIKES

By mid-1967, new American and ARVN strongpoints and camps had been built to oppose NVA and VC movements along the Laos and Cambodia borders. U.S. Special Forces troops were stationed in rural areas to train local militias in self-defense.

NVA general Giap was planning a general uprising for the South Vietnamese cities. Before then, he tried to bring U.S. forces into action at the borders, far from the cities. Attacks drew U.S. troops to reinforce the outposts at Khe Sanh and Con Thien. In October 1967 a Special Forces camp at Loc Ninh was hit. South Vietnamese reinforcements rushed in to save it.

Trained by U.S. advisors, the ARVN was clearly improving.

As other "border battles" continued, NVA and VC troops gathered around a Special Forces camp at Dak To in the rugged Central Highlands. Learning of the threat, General Creighton W. Abrams sent troops of the U.S. Fourth Division, the 173rd Airborne Brigade, and six ARVN battalions into action. Abrams was acting U.S. commander because Westmoreland was visiting Washington, D.C.

A series of firefights opened the contest at Dak To, and U.S. troops built "fire bases"—defensive positions.

DENSE FOREST
Close-quarters jungle fighting on steep terrain went on for three weeks near Dak To in November 1967. These weary troopers of the Fourth Battalion, 503rd Airborne Regiment, fought to capture Hill 875.

Losses	
U.S.:	289 killed
NVA:	1,644 killed
ARVN:	73 killed

The Americans attacked several fortified hilltops, driving out determined enemy defenders. This was some of the fiercest fighting of the war. To defend their retreat, the NVA occupied Hill 875. Troopers of the 503rd Airborne Regiment attacked the hill on November 19, meeting automatic-weapons fire and grenades. They found themselves in the midst of a network of tunnels, bunkers, and trenches. The battle continued day after day. Troopers were supported by tremendous air strikes that covered the hilltop with burning napalm—a flammable jelly contained in a bomb.

At last, on November 22—Thanksgiving Day—Hill 875 fell. The paratroopers had been without food or water for 50 hours.

Giap's plan to draw the Americans away from the cities did not succeed.

When his uprising began in January 1968, American troops were rapidly airlifted to the point of conflict.

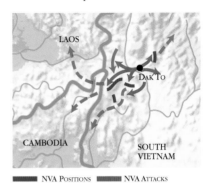

| NVA POSITIONS | NVA ATTACKS |
| NVA RETREATS | U.S. AND ARVN ATTACKS |

BATTLE FOR DAK TO
A handful of Special Forces advisors and a local militia company held their besieged camp at Dak To, while U.S. and ARVN troops defeated NVA soldiers who had surrounded the remote base.

THE LEADERSHIP

LT. GENERAL WILLIAM B. ROSSON commanded U.S. I Field Force, which was responsible for the Dak To area. Colonel Richard H. Johnson had operational command of part of the battle. He flew in a helicopter, attracting heavy enemy fire as he gave orders.

"The border battles were North Vietnamese failures."
—General Phillip B. Davidson, MACV chief of intelligence

JAMES H. JOHNSON
Lieutenant Colonel Johnson commanded the Fourth Battalion of the 503rd Airborne Regiment. He led his men through head-high grass and around jagged outcrops to find the enemy. Johnson alerted his company commanders that the battalion might be outnumbered two to one.

"Grab [the enemy] by the belt and thus avoid casualties from the artillery and air."
—NVA colonel Nguyen Huu An, on close-fighting tactics

HOANG MINH THAO
(born 1921)
From 1967 to late in the war, General Thao was commander of the military zone that the North Vietnamese called the Tay Nguyen Front. This was part of their Military Region 5 and included the Central Highlands, where Dak To was located, and also areas of northeastern Cambodia.

The War Reaches a Turning Point

The North Vietnamese and Viet Cong carefully planned an offensive they hoped would lead to a widespread uprising in South Vietnam. In January 1968, the country erupted in violence.

This was termed the "Tet Offensive" because it began during Tet, the Vietnamese New Year. More than 70,000 attackers, mostly VC, struck 100 cities and towns. Government troops and buildings and U.S. forces were assaulted. The cities of Saigon and Hué were especially hard hit.

General William Westmoreland, commander of MACV, was in the United States at the time. He was telling Congress and President Johnson the war was going well. Although he had 473,000 Americans "in country," Westmoreland asked for 200,000 more. He would not get them. Johnson was

A TET CASUALTY
Keeping low to avoid enemy fire, a marine drags a wounded buddy to safety. They are surrounded by the ruins of the Imperial Citadel's outer wall during the bloody battle for Hué in February 1968. The Tet Offensive opened in 1968, warning of much more fighting to come.

SIEGE OF KHE SANH
Oily smoke rises from a burning fuel depot hit during a Viet Cong rocket attack at the isolated U.S. Marine base at Khe Sanh in early 1968. Several hundred 122-mm rockets pounded the base in one day, blowing up the ammunition dump and the fuel supplies.

January	March	April	May
Siege of Khe Sanh begins	Siege of Hué ends	Siege of Khe Sanh ends	Peace talks begin in Paris
Tet Offensive is launched	Battle for Saigon ends		
Siege of Hué begins	Johnson announces he will not run for second term		
Battle for Saigon begins			

losing confidence in a military victory. As the conflict dragged on, disagreement over how to conduct the war deepened between the military and LBJ's administration.

The Tet Offensive was a turning point because it stirred up antiwar opposition in the United States. Under intense pressure, LBJ was unsure of the right course to follow. In March, he announced he would not run for a second term as president. Next, he called for peace talks, which formally began in Paris that spring.

Westmoreland left Vietnam in the summer to become army chief of staff, and General Creighton W. Abrams took command of MACV.

Campaigning with the promise that he would put an end to the war, Republican Richard M. Nixon was elected president in November.

TUNNEL RATS

There was no more dangerous duty than being the first to enter an enemy tunnel. Those courageous men who volunteered for this mission were nicknamed "tunnel rats." Armed with only a pistol and a flashlight, the soldier was lowered into the tunnel. He moved into the narrow chamber below, watching for signs of the enemy. He often had to avoid booby traps set to injure anyone who entered without permission. Explosives then were used to destroy the tunnel networks. There were so many tunnels, however, that they could not all be found.

AT THE ENTRANCE
An army engineer with pistol and flashlight carefully examines the opening to a Viet Cong tunnel in the town of Phu Hoa Dong.

July	October	November	December
Abrams replaces Westmoreland as commander of MACV	Johnson ends bombing of North Vietnam	Nixon wins presidential election	U.S. troop levels reach 495,000

GIAP HOPES FOR AN UPRISING

In mid-January 1968, North Vietnamese troops and Viet Cong prepared to launch a coordinated attack across South Vietnam. General Giap hoped to inspire the South Vietnamese people to revolt against their government. He also believed that a major uprising would convince the Americans that they were not winning the war.

For months, the NVA and VC had been secretly preparing this offensive. Guerrilla fighters entered the cities, where weapons had been cached, and waited for the moment to attack. Thousands of NVA troops took positions hidden in the jungle near American and ARVN bases.

Before the main attack was to start, Giap ordered his forces to open hostilities in regions far from the cities. The NVA began to besiege the large U.S. Marine base of Khe Sanh on January 21. Giap hoped to draw U.S. and ARVN troops away from the towns the VC planned to strike at the end of January.

The main Communist offensive exploded across the country on January 30. This was the Vietnamese New Year, known as "Tet." VC guerrillas appeared in more than 100 cities and towns, including Saigon.

THE LEADERSHIP

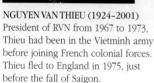

THE TET OFFENSIVE WAS PLANNED BY NVA general Vo Nguyen Giap, who expected ARVN forces to crumble. Instead, they fought well during Tet. American general Frederick C. Weyand had sensed trouble coming and doubled his force in Saigon, saving the city.

"We did our best to avoid malicious damage. Yet, when we had to destroy a house, we destroyed it."
—Marine captain Myron Harrington, on retaking Hué

NGUYEN VAN THIEU (1924-2001)
President of RVN from 1967 to 1973, Thieu had been in the Vietminh army before joining French colonial forces. Thieu fled to England in 1975, just before the fall of Saigon.

"Making an impact in the United States…had not been our intention—but it turned out to be a fortunate result."
—Tran Do, on Tet's unexpectedly powerful effect on America

TRAN DO (1923-2002)
Deputy commander of Communist forces in South Vietnam, Do was a key leader in the Tet offensive. The Communist Party expelled Do in 1998 after he called for more political freedom in Vietnam.

There, a guerrilla suicide team broke into the American embassy and fought to the death. Every American and ARVN base came under attack. The hardest fighting occurred in the northern city of Hué. There, the battle lasted 25 days before the Communists were defeated. By then, American and ARVN forces had recovered control of South Vietnam's other cities and towns.

MAJOR BATTLES OF THE TET OFFENSIVE

TET OFFENSIVE
Surprise VC attacks erupted all over South Vietnam in January 1968, with most uprisings occurring around the capital, Saigon. South Vietnamese cities and U.S. and ARVN military bases were attacked. The city of Hué saw some of the bloodiest and longest fighting.

The Tet Offensive did not cause a South Vietnamese uprising, but it cost the Communists extremely heavy casualties—at least 45,000 VC alone. U.S. MACV headquarters estimated the VC had lost the best of their fighters. Yet, Tet succeeded in troubling the American people, who had thought the war was almost over. Tet proved the VC and North Vietnamese were determined to fight on harder than ever.

Ammunition magazine

ARVN TROOPS IN BATTLE
South Vietnamese soldiers are on the alert for enemy fighters while their radioman, right, communicates with commanders during the Tet Offensive in 1968.

AMERICAN M-16 ASSAULT RIFLE
The M-16 was the standard rifle for U.S. forces in Vietnam. Designed in 1953, the M-16 was not as accurate as earlier weapons, but was lighter and fired much faster.

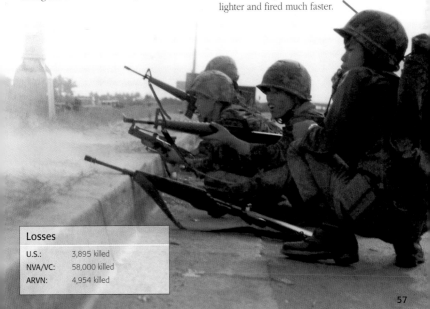

Losses	
U.S.:	3,895 killed
NVA/VC:	58,000 killed
ARVN:	4,954 killed

THE STRUGGLE FOR HUÉ

Most of the Tet fighting was over within a few days, as U.S. and government troops swiftly counterattacked. In the northern city of Hué, however, battles raged until March 2. Other cities had been attacked mainly by local VC, but Hué was occupied by a strong force of 7,500 NVA regulars. They took the district known as the New City and also fortified themselves within the walls of the Imperial Citadel. This fortress was in the beautiful old part of Hué, which once had been the Vietnamese capital.

ARVN general Ngo Quang Truong led his First Division in the defense of his headquarters, located in the Citadel. Reinforcing ARVN troops and U.S. airborne, marines, and infantry fought their way into the city. Block by block, they slowly cleared out the enemy fighters.

Soon after moving into Hué, the Communists began arresting and murdering local officials, military officers, westerners, and Christians. More than 2,800 people were murdered, and another 3,000 went missing. In their turn, ARVN forces executed anyone they thought was a Communist sympathizer.

U.S. and ARVN troops battled house to house as NVA troops stubbornly held their ground. Naval guns fired from offshore to support the

THE LEADERSHIP

HIS TWO MARINE REGIMENTS based eight miles from Hué were not at full strength, but Marine general Foster C. Lahue rushed them to the city. Lahue's marines recaptured a key wall of the Citadel and raised the Stars and Stripes.

"The [Tet] offensive served as the decisive blow...shaking the will of aggression of the U.S. imperialists."
—Communist Vietnamese postwar historian

LE VAN THAN
Colonel Than was the mayor of Hué and chief executive of Thua Thien Province, which surrounds the city. A native of the North, Than was key to Hué's reconstruction after Tet.

"[The] struggle for Hué was...possibly, the longest and bloodiest single action of the...war."
—*Washington Post*'s Donald Oberdorfer, who witnessed the battle

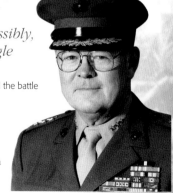

ERNEST C. CHEATHAM (born 1929)
Colonel Cheatham led his Second Battalion of the Fifth Marine Regiment into Hué to clear government buildings of the enemy. The marines were used to jungle fighting, not battling through narrow alleys. Ten days of conflict were needed to defeat the attackers. Cheatham is pictured after the war, as a general.

counterattacks. Heavy strikes by warplanes and artillery destroyed NVA strongpoints, and half of Hué was blasted into rubble. More than 100,000 inhabitants were made homeless by the fighting, which wound down by February 24.

Before 1968, it seemed the South Vietnamese cities were safe from attack, and General Westmoreland had declared that the war was being won. The Tet explosion, however, showed the enemy could attack anywhere. On the battlefield, Tet proved a defeat for the Communists. Because of its impact on American public opinion, however, Tet was a political victory for North Vietnam.

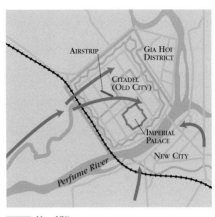

▬▬ MAIN NVA ATTACKS

HUÉ FALLS

NVA attackers held much of the Imperial Citadel and the New City before they were defeated. *Time* magazine wrote: "The battling turned the once-beautiful city into a nightmare."

HOUSE-TO-HOUSE FIGHTING

Men of the Fifth marine Regiment take cover behind a blown-out wall as U.S. artillery blasts an NVA position. After this "softening up" of the enemy, the marines resumed their push through Hué.

A CAPTURED FLAG

This cotton flag displays a gold star on a blue-and-red field. VC guerrillas carried the flag during fighting in 1968. Captured, it now rests in the collections of the U.S. Center of Military History.

Losses	
U.S.:	216 killed, 1,364 wounded
NVA/VC:	5,000 killed, 98 taken prisoner
ARVN:	384 killed, 1,830 wounded

VIET CONG RAID EMBASSY

The most important battle of the Tet Offensive was the U.S. and ARVN defense of Saigon's Tan Son Nhut airfield, which housed MACV headquarters. The Communists sent 35 battalions into action against II Field Force, which defended the Saigon region. This unit included 50 U.S. battalions as well as ARVN and international troops. Eleven VC battalions struck at Saigon in the early morning darkness of January 31, 1968. As enemy assaults exploded everywhere, General Fred C. Weyand focused on defending Tan Son Nhut.

Commanding II Field Force, Weyand was ready for trouble. Military intelligence had warned that a major enemy operation was planned, so Weyand had drawn his forces closer to Saigon. As soon as the Tet Offensive began, Weyand's own headquarters at the Long Binh military base also came under attack. While

RUBBER SANDALS
The NVA were more lightly equipped than U.S. and ARVN troops. These NVA sandals were ideal for Vietnam's hot, watery environment. They dried quickly and kept the wearer cool. The soles are made of old tires.

THE LEADERSHIP

FLYING IN A HELICOPTER above the battlefield, Colonel Glenn K. Otis directed his Fourth Cavalry squadron in the crucial counterattack that drove the VC away from Tan Son Nhut. This was the decisive victory of the Tet Offensive.

"We went to Vietnam in the first place to assist the South Vietnamese people—not to defeat the North Vietnamese."

—Weyand, on U.S. reasons for the war

FREDERICK C. WEYAND (born 1916)
Commander of the Twenty-fifth Infantry Division, Weyand headed II Field Force until July 1968. In 1972 he took command of MACV, replacing Creighton Abrams. Weyand was highly regarded by his subordinates. In 1975, however, he underestimated the U.S. financial commitment needed to support South Vietnam against Hanoi.

"Everything was for the common cause. One for all, all for one."
—Tran Van Tra, quoted after the war

TRAN VAN TRA (1918-1996)
A former Vietminh officer, Tra commanded the Communist effort in the lower half of South Vietnam. He helped plan Tet and led the assault on Saigon. After the war, Tra publicly criticized the Hanoi high command.

defending Long Binh, he ordered a counterattack led by armor (tanks) that drove off enemy forces assaulting Tan Son Nhut. He also airlifted troops to protect the U.S. Embassy in Saigon, where government buildings were in danger.

A VC platoon of 19 men had entered the embassy grounds, but had been wiped out after a few hours. Americans were shocked to see television news coverage of the embassy attack. If Tan Son Nhut and MACV headquarters had fallen, the VC would have won a major victory.

Fighting for Saigon was mainly over by February 5, although ARVN troops continued cleaning up enemy resistance until March 7. Thanks to Weyand's leadership, Saigon was

SAIGON BATTLE
VC attacks in January turned Saigon into a battlefield. General Weyand led the defense of Saigon, including his Long Binh headquarters and MACV's headquarters at Tan Son Nhut airfield.

▬▬▬ VIET CONG ATTACKS

▬▬▬ U.S. AND ARVN ATTACKS

saved. Yet it now seemed to many Americans that the ongoing struggle in Vietnam was a bloody stalemate with no end in sight. Opposition to the war now grew much stronger.

DEMANDING SURRENDER
ARVN soldiers call for trapped Viet Cong fighters to give up during Tet Offensive fighting in Saigon. Many who did surrender were executed on the spot. Television footage of one such killing caused an uproar when shown in the United States.

Losses

U.S.:	110 killed/wounded
VC:	1,100 killed/wounded

ANOTHER SMALL HELL

The Vietminh siege of French-held Dien Bien Phu in 1954 was later called "hell in a very small place." In 1968, General Giap wished he could win another devastating victory just like Dien Bien Phu. The U.S. outpost at Khe Sanh, near the Demilitarized Zone, seemed the right target. Giap planned an artillery bombardment that would make Khe Sanh as hellish as Dien Bien Phu. For months, he secretly built up a 40,000-strong force within striking distance of the base.

Khe Sanh's 6,700 marines, ARVN rangers, and Special Forces troops protected Route 9, an important highway. They also blocked enemy movement from Laos toward the South Vietnamese coast. The NVA attacked them before dawn on January 21, launching hundreds of 122-mm rockets and an artillery barrage. Khe Sanh's ammunition dump took a direct hit and exploded.

The U.S. and ARVN outposts in the surrounding hills were also struck by the NVA, but they held out despite fierce pressure. Unlike at Dien Bien Phu, Giap was not allowed control of the heights around Khe Sanh. Also,

THE LEADERSHIP

FIELD CONFERENCE
NVA and VC officers plan battle tactics on a table laid out in their jungle camp near the Demilitarized Zone (DMZ) in December 1967. The Tet Offensive involved NVA assaults on remote bases such as Khe Sanh, just below the DMZ.

WESTMORELAND AND THIEU believed taking Khe Sanh was the main Tet objective. Many historians believe the siege was meant to tie down U.S. manpower, and that holding the base was a waste of resources.

"[The NVA are] fresh, well-equipped troops with new haircuts and good morale...not a rabble but a well-trained force."
—Marine general Carl W. Hoffman, about Khe Sanh

"I see no requirement to change our strategy."
—Westmoreland, on Tet's military influence

U.S. COMMANDERS
Marine colonel David E. Lownds, center, commanded Khe Sanh combat base during the 1968 siege. Here he confers with Chaplain John W. McElroy, left, and visiting general Victor R. Krulak. Lownds was a veteran of World War II and the Korean War.

unlike the French, whose air power was weak, the Americans at Khe Sanh had tremendous air support. During the 77-day siege, warplanes dropped more than 100,000 tons (90.7 million kg) of bombs and rockets onto NVA positions. Devastating B-52 heavy bombing inflicted severe casualties, helping prevent the NVA from mounting direct attacks on the defenses. Still, an average of 2,500 enemy rounds hit the base each week. Khe Sanh was less than 2,000 yards (1,800 m) long and 900 yards (810 m) wide.

MACV sent 15,000 troops to reinforce the Route 9 outposts. Another 50,000 went into action throughout the region, with the First Cavalry Division (Airmobile) battling toward Khe Sanh. First Cav troopers fought their way through to the hilltop base on April 8, ending the siege.

NORTH VIETNAM

DMZ (DEMILITARIZED ZONE)

KHE SANH

QUANG TRI

SOUTH VIETNAM

LAOS

▬▬▬ NVA ATTACKS
▬▬▬ U.S. AND ARVN OPERATIONS

KHE SANH

The remote Khe Sanh combat base was besieged from all sides. U.S. and ARVN forces fought hard to clear the hills surrounding the marine base, and 24,000 air strikes pounded the enemy's positions.

RVN FLAG

As the war progressed, the valor of ARVN forces won honors for the flag of South Vietnam. For centuries, the Vietnamese have been courageous soldiers who fought for their homeland.

UP IN SMOKE

More than 1,500 tons (1.3 million kg) of munitions and fuel were lost in the first NVA rocket barrage on Khe Sanh. Dense black smoke from burning supplies and secondary explosions covered the combat base.

Losses

U.S.:	291 killed, 1,459 wounded
NVA:	10,000–15,000 killed
ARVN:	34 killed, 184 wounded

A HIDDEN, DEADLY WAR

The effort to "pacify" South Vietnam required establishing security in the villages. Even when U.S. or ARVN forces did drive the enemy out, there were not enough troops to stay behind and garrison the many villages. In 1967, the U.S. military, civilian aid agencies, and intelligence organizations joined forces to carry out the pacification effort. They established the Civil Operations and Revolutionary Development Support (CORDS) organization.

Headed by civilian Robert W. Komer, CORDS coordinated the efforts of several hundred civilian-military pacification teams around South Vietnam. CORDS provided training and arms for village self-defense and also aided in such tasks as reconstruction and development of local water resources.

Following the Tet Offensive, the CIA began a new campaign to overcome VC influence among the rural population. This was the Phoenix Program, designed to identify and kill or arrest Communist agents and supporters in the villages. Springing from CORDS, the Phoenix Program had killed at least 20,500 persons and arrested 29,000 more by 1972. Much of the effort was in

The sphinx of Thebes, Egypt, symbolizes wisdom and silence.

U.S. INTELLIGENCE PATCH
This patch was worn on the shoulder of U.S. intelligence officers in Vietnam. The patch shows the sphinx of Thebes, Egypt, over a yellow map of Vietnam. The sphinx is the symbol of U.S. Army military intelligence.

ENEMY FLAG
A "Provincial Reconnaissance Unit" examines a VC flag discovered in the Mekong Delta. Part of the Phoenix Program, these units worked in counter-espionage. They carried out arrests and assassinations of accused Communist leaders and sympathizers in the rural countryside.

Losses	
VC:	estimated 20,000–40,000 killed, 29,000 prisoners

AREAS OF PREDOMINANTLY VIET CONG-HELD VILLAGES

MEKONG DELTA
The vast Mekong Delta region was a base of Viet Cong support. The Phoenix Program did much of its work here until dangers from the 1972 Communist offensive forced it to come to a halt.

the swampy Mekong Delta, where the VC had strong support. Civilian Robert E. Colby later took over as CORDS director and ran Phoenix.

Termed an "assassination program" by its critics, Phoenix had severe faults. For one, the police and military often were given false information, so innocent persons became their victims. Also, Phoenix personnel had quotas to make sure they worked hard. Too often, innocent persons were killed or arrested just to fill those quotas. Corrupt soldiers and police took bribes—often from real VC agents who were then released. Helpless civilians were caught between the government and VC. Neither hesitated to torture and kill civilians.

After the war, Communist statements admitted the Phoenix Program did, in fact, greatly damage VC influence over the villages.

THE LEADERSHIP

WHEN KOMER BEGAN CORDS, the VC controlled 60 percent of the RSV countryside. Many U.S. advisors despised Phoenix because it hurt villagers. Captain Stuart Herrington said, "No single endeavor caused such grief and frustration [for advisors like myself]."

"Those killings occurred mostly in combat situations. . . ."
—Colby, on the Phoenix death toll

WILLIAM E. COLBY (1920-1996)
A veteran of World War II covert operations run by the OSS, Colby had experience working with civilian resistance fighters in Europe. After the Vietnam War, Colby went on to become director of the CIA from 1974 to 1975.

TRUONG CHINH (1907-1988)
A key member of Hanoi's Politburo—political leadership—Chinh pushed for a total military victory. The conflict was known to Hanoi leaders as "the special war." Victory required political control of South Vietnam's villages despite the influence of the Phoenix Program.

"Phoenix was a devious and cruel [operation that cost] the loss of thousands of our cadres."
—Colonel Bui Tin, a Viet Cong senior officer

Secret Bombings and Massacre at My Lai

President Nixon took office with a campaign promise to bring peace to Vietnam. Many hoped Nixon was right when he said that his plan would end the war and bring American troops home.

In 1969, Nixon called for South Vietnam to be strengthened enough to defend itself against the NVA and VC. This "Vietnamization" of the war would allow U.S. troops to leave, but it would take years. Meanwhile more troops were deployed. U.S. force numbers reached their highest level of the war in April, with 543,000 Americans serving in Vietnam.

On March 18, Nixon began Operation Menu, the bombing of NVA bases in neutral Cambodia. Throughout the war, enemy forces had retreated into Cambodia to regroup. The MACV commander, General Creighton Abrams, requested the bombings to destroy the NVA

UNSEEN ENEMY
A soldier of the U.S. Ninth Infantry Division watches for danger as he wades through an irrigation ditch. This action took place in the steamy summer heat of the Mekong Delta, southwest of Saigon, in 1969.

March	April	May	June
Operation Menu begins	U.S. troop levels reach 543,000, the highest of the war	Assault on Ap Bia Mountain is the last large-scale U.S. engagement of the war	U.S. troop withdrawals begin

sanctuaries. Bombing a neutral country was against international law, and Nixon kept it secret.

In May, a bloody U.S. assault on NVA positions at Ap Bia Mountain did come to public attention, causing an outcry. Nixon ordered General Abrams to avoid further costly battles. In June, the first troop withdrawals began, with 25,000 soldiers sent home.

That September, a U.S. military court charged Lieutenant William Calley with the massacre of hundreds of unarmed civilians in the village of My Lai. With such terrible revelations, many more Americans became disillusioned with the war. In October more than 250,000 protesters came to Washington, D.C. Many thousands more gathered in other cities. Ho Chi Minh died in September at the age of 79. Power passed to leaders Le Duan, Pham Van Dong, and Vo Nguyen Giap.

BROWN WATER NAVY

"Brown Water Navy" was a nickname for the U.S. Army-Navy forces that patrolled the many rivers and lakes of South Vietnam. Beginning in 1965, the U.S. Navy's River Patrol Force had this task. They were joined by the Mobile Riverine Force in 1967. The riverine forces, supported by the South Vietnamese Navy, controlled the waterways, including the strategic Mekong Delta. Admiral Elmo Zumwalt Jr., commander U.S. Naval Forces, Vietnam, conducted riverine operations at their height in 1968. Zumwalt praised his sailors, saying the "tales of their courage are legend."

A BRIEF REST
U.S. servicemen share a relaxed moment aboard a gunboat on the My Tho River in July 1969. When they were on patrol duty deeper in enemy territory, their situation was dangerous and tense.

ALERT FOR SNIPERS
U.S. soldiers looking for the enemy in the swamplands south of Saigon turn toward the sound of firing from a hidden sniper. They are moving away from peasant huts in Vietnam's agricultural delta lands. Here, thousands of VC fighters and their officers kept a firm grip on the villagers.

September	October	November	December
Ho Chi Minh dies	More than 250,000 antiwar protesters march in Washington, D.C	Nixon gives a speech asking Americans to support his policies in Vietnam	Number of troops killed in Vietnam reaches 40,024
Lieutenant Calley charged with murdering unarmed civilians at My Lai			

UNLAWFUL BOMBING

In the past, VC and NVA forces had escaped American air and ground attacks by crossing the border from Vietnam to their bases in neutral Cambodia. The United States honored Cambodia's neutrality, and

> *"We are not fighting for terrain as such. We are going after the enemy."*
> —General Creighton Abrams

therefore U.S. troops did not follow. To overcome this disadvantage, the MACV commander, General Creighton Abrams, requested permission from President Nixon to bomb enemy bases in Cambodia. On March 18, Nixon authorized Operation Menu, keeping it secret from Congress. B-52 heavy bombers flew 3,875 missions against enemy bases. In May 1970 the *New York Times* revealed the illegal operation, but when there was no wide public outcry, Nixon continued bombing. Menu went on until 1973, when peace was signed with North Vietnam.

✳ OPERATION MENU TARGETS
▨ HO CHI MINH TRAIL
▪▪▪▪ SIHANOUK TRAIL
▬ U.S. ATTACK ON HO CHI MINH TRAIL

ATTACKING SUPPLIES
Operation Menu bombing attacks were coordinated with ground offensives. The end of the Ho Chi Minh Trail was hard hit.

THE LEADERSHIP

OPERATION MENU WAS UNOFFICIALLY approved by Cambodia's Prince Sihanouk. A vote by the U.S. Congress finally ended the bombing in August 1973. By then, 383,800 tons (350 million kg) of bombs had been dropped.

CREIGHTON W. ABRAMS (1914–1974)
General Abrams served as MACV commander from 1968 to 1972. He carried out Johnson's plan to limit troop strength in Vietnam, and was directed to reduce U.S. casualties by ending of large-unit operations.

STRAFING RUN
This overhead view shows a U.S. Air Force F-100 fighter-bomber's attack in the So San area of Cambodia in May 1970. The warplane has already dropped its bombs. Operation Menu aimed to destroy enemy supply routes and storage bases on the Ho Chi Minh Trail.

Statistics

383,800 tons (350 million kg) of bombs dropped on Cambodia

3,875 B-52 bombing raids from March 1969 to May 1970

DEATH ON AP BIA

Helicopters carried 101st Airborne troopers into the strategic A Shau Valley near the Laotian border on May 10. They attacked NVA positions on Ap Bia Mountain, sparking a ten-day battle. A combined U.S. and ARVN assault captured Ap Bia, but 46 U.S. troops died, with 400 wounded. Believing they had been sent into a "meat grinder" of enemy fire, the troopers named Ap Bia "Hamburger Hill." Americans at home were furious that Ap Bia was soon abandoned. Nixon ordered General Abrams to avoid large-scale engagements like Hamburger Hill in the future. Abrams was to concentrate on strengthening the ARVN, in preparation for U.S. troop withdrawals.

> *"[Honeycutt] won't stop until he kills every one of us."*
>
> —Wounded 101st Airborne trooper, quoted by a news correspondent

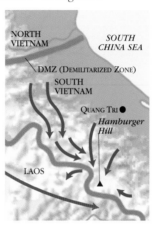

NORTH VIETNAM

SOUTH CHINA SEA

DMZ (DEMILITARIZED ZONE)

SOUTH VIETNAM

QUANG TRI ●

Hamburger Hill

LAOS

▬▬▬ HO CHI MINH TRAIL

▬▬▬ U.S. AND ARVN OPERATIONS JANUARY–MAY 1969

HIGH PEAK

The 3,000-foot (914 m) Ap Bia Mountain dominated the strategic A Shau Valley, which was a corridor for enemy invasions. The battle for Ap Bia was the end of major U.S. ground operations in the Vietnam War.

THE LEADERSHIP

GENERAL ABRAMS SUPERVISED the "Vietnamization" of the war. He conducted offensive operations in early 1969, but heavy U.S. losses were unacceptable to Nixon.

WELDON F. HONEYCUTT

Commander of a paratrooper battalion, Colonel Honeycutt enraged his men with repeated attacks. Angry soldiers later offered $10,000 to whoever killed Honeycutt. He survived the war.

INTO ACTION

Paratroopers leap from a helicopter in the capture of Hamburger Hill, above the A Shau Valley. When U.S. troops withdrew, soldiers and civilians questioned why the bloody battle had been necessary.

Losses	
U.S.:	46 killed, 400 wounded
NVA:	633 killed

69

Vietnamization and Cambodian Invasion

By the start of 1970, more than 40,000 Americans had been killed and 260,000 wounded in Vietnam. Public opinion in the United States was steadily turning against the war.

President Nixon called for the South Vietnamese Army to be strengthened and do more of the fighting. This "Vietnamization" of the war would allow more Americans to be withdrawn. The American public thought the war was winding down. Early in the year, Nixon began secret peace talks with Hanoi. Then he ordered an increased bombing campaign to weaken the Communists. He also invaded Cambodia in April to destroy enemy bases and supply routes. This angered those Americans who had thought the war would end soon.

There was a new round of antiwar protests, especially on college campuses. In May, Ohio National

SOLDIERS FIRE ON STUDENTS
This Pulitzer prize–winning photo appeared on the cover of *Newsweek* magazine, May 18, 1970, with the title "Nixon's Home Front." Shown dead on the ground is one of the four students killed when National Guardsmen fired on antiwar protesters at Kent State University in Ohio.

February 1970	April	May	June
Heavy airstrikes by B-52 bombers on the Ho Chi Minh Trail	Nixon authorizes invasion of Cambodia	Four students killed in antiwar protest at Kent State University	Senate repeals Gulf of Tonkin Resolution
Kissinger begins secret peace talks in Paris	U.S. troops enter Cambodia to attack Viet Cong there	Two students killed at Jackson State College	U.S. combat troops withdraw from Cambodia

Guardsmen fired on student demonstrators at Kent State University in Ohio. Four students were killed and several wounded. Two students at Jackson State College in Mississippi were also killed during antiwar protests.

In June, the U.S. Senate voted to repeal the 1964 Gulf of Tonkin Resolution that had allowed the president to wage war in Vietnam. Nixon no longer had a free hand to widen the war or increase bombing

The United States kept reducing its forces in Vietnam. By the end of 1970, approximately 280,000 Americans were serving there. In 1971, there were no major American ground actions, but the air force was active, bombing the North and supporting ARVN operations. Almost 140,000 more troops were withdrawn during 1971. Still, the war continued.

STRIFE IN CAMBODIA
Cambodian government soldiers using outdated rifles find cover as they come under heavy fire. They are fighting Cambodian Communist guerrillas who are allied with North Vietnam and the VC.

VIETNAMIZATION

When large numbers of U.S. troops came to Vietnam, it was termed "Americanization" of the war. "Vietnamization" called for strengthening South Vietnam's military as the Americans gradually left. Since this required many more troops, South Vietnam began to draft all men ages 17 to 43. In addition, the United States gave the ARVN better equipment and training. By 1970, ARVN soldiers were more confident and fought harder on the battlefield. Yet the South Vietnamese government still needed American military support to oppose North Vietnam.

WAITING FOR HELICOPTERS
Soldiers of the South Vietnamese Army prepare to be airlifted by American helicopters for an operation near the Cambodian border.

October	November	January 1971	December
Nixon proposes cease-fire, Hanoi does not respond	Trial begins of Lt. William Calley for responsibility in My Lai massacre	ARVN launches Lam Son 719, an attack into Laos	U.S. troop levels drop to 156,800
ARVN forces begin two new drives into Cambodia			

WIDENING THE WAR

Earlier in the Vietnam conflict, General Westmoreland's request to enter neutral Cambodia or Laos to attack enemy bases and supply lines had been refused by President Johnson. Invading a small, neutral country would have damaged U.S. honor and prestige and further inflamed the antiwar movement. By 1970, however, President Nixon was desperate to force North Vietnam to make peace. Nixon also wanted to blunt enemy attempts to take advantage of the withdrawal of U.S. forces from Vietnam. Therefore, he now approved invading Cambodia.

Secret bombing of NVA positions in Cambodia had been going on for a year. In March, pro-U.S. Cambodian general Lon Nol had deposed Prince Sihanouk, Cambodia's neutralist head of state. General Nol's government was under attack from Cambodian "Khmer Rouge" guerrillas.

In April, ARVN troops crossed into "the Parrot's Beak" area of Cambodia, and U.S. and ARVN forces later entered "the Fishhook." These regions held enemy sanctuaries and supply routes that threatened Saigon itself.

On April 30, Nixon publicly

A HEAVY HAUL
South Vietnamese troops collect enemy munitions— land mines, mortar rounds, and rockets—captured in May 1970 from the Parrot's Beak area of Cambodia. Despite such losses, the NVA and VC rebuilt their bases soon after U.S. and ARVN forces left.

SPIT SHINE
U.S. Army combat boots were highly polished to look smart. Compared to light NVA and VC footwear, boots were bulky and soaked up water. The difference between heavy army boots and rubber-and-canvas NVA footwear reflected each side's fighting style.

Losses	
U.S.:	338 killed, 1,525 wounded
NVA/VC:	11,000 killed, 2,500 prisoners
ARVN:	638 killed, 3,009 wounded

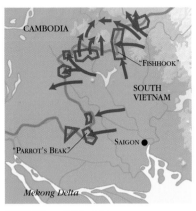

U.S. AND ARVN ATTACKS

VC AND NVA BORDER SANCTUARIES

CAMBODIAN INCURSIONS
Taking the war to the enemy, 20,000 U.S. and ARVN troops, supported by air strikes, thrust into Cambodia. The forests of the region concealed enemy supply routes and base camps that now were destroyed.

announced this "cross-border incursion," as a brief invasion is termed.

The Fishhook was overwhelmed by 15,000 U.S. troops, who found only abandoned NVA bases. After a tough fight in the Parrot's Beak, 8,700 U.S. and ARVN soldiers drove out the enemy. The NVA and Khmer Rouge strategy was to retreat in the face of an advancing superior force, then return when it began to withdraw. Other raids into Cambodia occurred along the border, and large quantities of arms and munitions were captured.

By July, U.S. troops had withdrawn, leaving only ARVN in Cambodia. A looming NVA offensive had been set back by the invasion, and pressure on Lon Nol's anti-communist government was temporarily relieved.

THE LEADERSHIP

GENERAL DO CAO TRI LED THE ARVN drive into "the Parrot's Beak," and General Robert Shoemaker commanded a U.S. and ARVN attack on "the Fishhook." Both areas jutted into South Vietnam.

"We take this action...for the purpose of ending the war in Vietnam."
—Nixon, justifying the Cambodian invasion

RICHARD M. NIXON (1913-1994)
Nixon had originally been a strong supporter of the Vietnam conflict. As president, he worked to get the United States out without appearing defeated. Threatened with impeachment for covering up political scandals, he resigned in August 1974.

"[Cambodia] can no longer tolerate the seizure of...territory by the Viet Cong [and] North Vietnam. They must go."
—Lon Nol, April 1970

LON NOL (1913-1985)
Defense minister Nol overthrew Prince Sihanouk in March 1973. Nol blamed Sihanouk for allowing the NVA and VC to use Cambodia for bases and supply lines. As prime minister, Nol led a corrupt government, which was ousted by Cambodian Communists in 1975.

RETREAT INTO ROUT

The invasion of Laos began in late January 1971, but American ground troops were not permitted to take part. After the 1970 Cambodian invasion, Congress had forbidden American ground troops to attack across borders. The Laos ground invasion was an ARVN operation, but it was supported by U.S. helicopters, warplanes, and artillery bombardments.

Led by ARVN general Hoang Xuan Lam, the invasion was code-named Lam Son 719. It aimed to destroy important NVA base areas and weapons caches and block the Ho Chi Minh Trail. Up to 21,000 South Vietnamese airborne, rangers, and marine troops were involved. This was their chance to test the success of the "Vietnamization" of the war. On February 8, ARVN troops and armor crossed the Laotian border to take the town of Aloui, 13 miles (21 km) along Route 9.

Heliborne operations quickly carried soldiers to landing zones, where forward firebases were established. The roads were bad, however, and columns of wheeled vehicles and armor often became bogged down. Much of the invasion

THE LEADERSHIP

CIVIL WAR RAGED IN LAOS, where the CIA funded Prince Souvanna Phouma's government army and a force of 25,000 local tribesmen. These fought the Communist Pathet Lao—led by the prince's half-brother, Souphanouvong—and the North Vietnamese Army.

"We will burn the old grass and the new will grow."

—Pol Pot, on his regime's murderous policies

POL POT (1928–1998)
One of several Communist leaders in Indochina, Pol Pot headed Cambodia's Khmer Rouge. He was hostile to Vietnamese Communists occupying territory in Cambodia and Laos. Gaining power in 1975, he killed millions of non-Communist Cambodians. The Vietnamese drove him out in 1978.

"The North Vietnamese had to oppose Lam Son 719 with every resource they could bring to bear."

—General Philip B. Davidson, on threatening NVA supply lines

HOANG XUAN LAM (born 1928)
Commander of the ARVN I Corps, General Lam recaptured Hué during the 1968 Tet fighting. In Lam Son 719, a nervous President Thieu stopped Lam's advance, giving the enemy time to regroup. Thieu replaced Lam following the NVA assault on Quang Tri in 1972.

LAM SON 719
More than 600 American helicopters supported the ARVN's swift drive across the border into Laos. Then President Thieu had his doubts in the face of stiff NVA counterattacks. Thieu ordered his outnumbered troops to withdraw, resulting in panic and the rout of ARVN forces.

VIET CONG POSITIONS AND ATTACKS

U.S. AIR ASSAULTS

ARVN PATCH
Lightning bolts, a leopard, and a parachute are symbols on this South Vietnamese Army Special Forces shoulder patch. U.S.-trained Rangers were expert paratroopers who admired the leopard's physical qualities.

force was strung out along Route 9, offering vulnerable targets. NVA counterattacks soon struck these columns and assaulted the forward firebases.

By March 12, ever-increasing enemy resistance forced General Lam to withdraw from his positions. The ARVN retreat along Route 9 began, and the NVA immediately moved to cut it off. The Communists inflicted casualties

WAITING TO LEAVE
Wounded South Vietnamese Rangers hope for a medevac (medical evacuation) helicopter to arrive soon at a landing zone near the Laotian border. ARVN soldiers who were soundly defeated at Lam Son in 1971 responded gallantly a year later and repulsed major NVA offensives.

and blew up ARVN vehicles. Damaged ARVN tanks blocked the road. The crews abandoned their trapped vehicles and fled on foot. Panic overtook many, and ARVN losses were heavy. Withdrawal turned into rout.

Operation Lam Son ended on April 6, a severe ARVN defeat. Further, the United States lost 100 helicopters, with another 618 damaged. "Vietnamization" was far from a success.

Losses
U.S.: 215 killed, 1,187 wounded/missing
NVA/VC: 20,000 killed/wounded
ARVN: 1,764 killed, 5,918 wounded/missing

NVA Offensive and B-52s for Peace

Relations between America and the Communist powers were changing in 1972. Talks with the Soviets aimed to slow the buildup of nuclear weapons, and President Nixon visited China.

North Vietnam was alarmed that its main allies were dealing with America. Hanoi's MiG fighter planes, surface-to-air missiles, guns, tanks, and oil came from the Soviet Union and China. The leadership in Hanoi decided they must unite North and South Vietnam before the major powers reached an agreement to end the war.

Commander in Chief Vo Nguyen Giap began the "Eastertide Offensive" on March 30. More than 125,000 troops, backed by tanks and heavy artillery, launched a three-pronged attack on South Vietnam.

South Vietnamese forces were at first driven back everywhere. Then President Thieu sent top ARVN

TOUGH NEGOTIATORS
After four years of on-again, off-again negotiations, the Paris Peace Talks continued into 1972. U.S. representative Henry Kissinger, left, talks through an interpreter with Hanoi's senior representative, Le Duc Tho, right. The U.S. wanted a mutual withdrawal of its and North Vietnam's troops from South Vietnam, but Hanoi objected to a divided Vietnam.

March 1972	April	May	June
Eastertide Offensive begins	NVA attacks Kontum	Quang Tri falls to NVA	Weyand replaces Abrams as commander of MACV
	NVA attacks An Loc	Operation Linebacker I begins	
	U.S. troop levels at 69,000	Attack on Kontum stopped	

generals to take command. In the north, with U.S. air support, the ARVN began to push back the enemy. The NVA offensives in the south and center of South Vietnam were also stopped with the aid of American air strikes.

As the battle for South Vietnam raged, American and North Vietnamese diplomats negotiated in Paris. When the peace process stalled, Nixon ordered new bombing of North Vietnam. For 11 days in December, B-52 bombers battered North Vietnamese cities. At the end of the year, North Vietnam agreed to continue negotiations.

The Paris Peace Accords were signed on January 27, 1973. By March, American troops were withdrawn in Operation Homecoming, and U.S. prisoners of war were returned. For the United States, the Second Indochina War had ended.

BOMBS AS PERSUASION
North Vietnam's Haiphong Harbor shudders under heavy U.S. bombing ordered by President Nixon in mid-1972. Nixon's Linebacker I and II massive bombing campaigns were intended to force Hanoi to agree to terms that would end hostilities. This severe destruction helped persuade the Communists to agree to a cease-fire in 1973.

OPERATION HOMECOMING

Most prisoners of war (POWs) were pilots, shot down on missions over North Vietnam. Many were held in the "Hanoi Hilton," their nickname for a grim prison in Hanoi. Though North Vietnam had signed the 1949 Geneva Convention—a treaty stating the rights of prisoners—it was ignored. Newly captured pilots were humiliated, forced to parade through Hanoi. Many men were tortured, and some were kept for years in solitary confinement. The POWs were finally released in "Operation Homecoming," which lasted from February through April 1973.

PRISONERS GOING HOME
Under guard, weary U.S. prisoners of war step from a bus that has taken them from their prison to Hanoi's Gia Lam Airport in 1973. They soon will fly to the Philippines, then on to the United States and home.

December	January 1973	March	August
Peace talks collapse	Paris Peace Accords signed	Operation Homecoming is completed	Operation Menu, secret bombing of Cambodia, ends
Linebacker II begins	U.S. to withdraw all troops in 60 days	Last U.S. troops leave Vietnam	
Peace talks resume			

THE ARVN VICTORIOUS

The war was not going as well as Hanoi would have liked by 1971. The Communists were losing influence over much of South Vietnam's countryside. The terrible Viet Cong losses during the Tet Offensive of 1968 had allowed Saigon to reclaim governmental control over villages. The government now dominated 35 out of 45 provinces. Americans were withdrawing, but South Vietnam's military had grown. It numbered more than one million and was well-armed and supplied by the United States. It appeared that time would only bring about a stronger South Vietnamese government. Hanoi's guerrilla warfare and limited counterattacks would not win final victory.

Now North Vietnam began turning its army into a heavier, more conventional fighting force with more tanks. By the end of 1971, the NVA was equipped with new tanks, artillery, and trucks—mostly provided by the Soviets. Preparations were made for a three-pronged invasion of the South. General Giap himself took over the operation and a force of 200,000 troops. One attack would push

THE LEADERSHIP

GIAP EMPLOYED WEAPONS SELDOM used by the NVA: Soviet T-54 tanks and heavy artillery. His troops gained valuable experience with armor, but the ARVN outfought them. NVA forces in South Vietnam grew from 80,000 in 1972 to 150,000 in 1974.

VO NGUYEN GIAP (born 1911)
The long, successful military career of General Giap came to a close with the 1972 offensive. His forces won much territory, but too many died, and the goal of defeating the ARVN was not achieved. Giap served as minister of national defense until 1980.

"A Western commander absorbing losses on the scale of Giap's would hardly have lasted."
—Westmoreland, after the war

"Quang Tri City could not have been retaken…had it not been for the support provided by the U.S. Air Force."
—General Truong

NGO QUANG TRUONG (born 1929)
General Truong led his ARVN First Infantry Division in key counterattacks at Hué in 1968. After stopping the 1972 offensive, Truong commanded ARVN forces in northern South Vietnam. He fought the 1975 NVA invasion, evacuating his remaining troops from Da Nang by sea.

through Quang Tri Province near the DMZ, and a second would drive into central South Vietnam. A third would strike from Cambodia toward Saigon. The main objectives were destroying the ARVN and causing an uprising to overthrow President Nguyen Van Thieu's government.

The offensive began at the DMZ on March 30, 1972, just before Easter. A massive artillery bombardment of ARVN bases was followed by 30,000 men and 200 tanks sweeping across the DMZ. The surprised ARVN infantry and armor were driven back but fought hard. The ARVN's best general, Ngo Quang Truong, took command of a counteroffensive at Quang Tri. Supported by U.S. air power and naval gunfire, General Truong pushed back the NVA in a struggle that raged on week after week.

Other battles continued at Kontum in central South Vietnam, and An Loc near Saigon. The ARVN defeated the Kontum and An Loc offensives by July. It took until September 16 for General Truong to turn back the Quang Tri offensive, routing six NVA divisions in his remarkable triumph.

NVA ATTACKS

THREE STROKES
Giap's forces had early success on all three fronts in 1972. The ARVN fought bravely with U.S. air support and repulsed the attacks. Giap was faulted for dividing his army and not being strong enough anywhere.

NVA INVASION
Preparing for the NVA offensive in April 1972, ARVN troops aboard an M-48 tank take a defensive position overlooking Route 9. They are north of Quang Tri, near Dong Ha. The invasion of this region would be stopped and driven back by September.

Losses	
NVA:	more than 100,000 killed/wounded
ARVN:	40,000 killed/wounded

DEFENDING SAIGON

ARVN forces backed by U.S. air power fought courageously against the massive Eastertide Offensive that began in March. Nowhere was the NVA threat more serious than north of Saigon. Here, the third prong of the offensive aimed to capture the city of An Loc, 45 miles (170 km) from Saigon. An Loc was to be turned into the official seat of the "Provisional Revolutionary Government of Vietnam." This would be a temporary capital for the Communists as they battled the Saigon government.

On April 6, NVA troops and armor surged out of Cambodia, hitting the ARVN hard. Defenders of the frontier town of Loc Ninh were wiped out by 25 NVA tanks swarming over them. Despite ferocious assaults, the South Vietnamese at An Loc were determined to hold out. NVA forces cut supply lines between Saigon and the ARVN forces in the field. Then the NVA experienced their own difficulties in waging conventional warfare. Their fast-advancing troops had to slow down to await resupply.

This gave President Thieu time to organize a counteroffensive. With U.S. air attacks in close support, ARVN airborne and infantry established strong defensive positions 30 miles (48 km) north of Saigon. Others reinforced An Loc, which came under siege. Meanwhile, NVA troops moved to within 15 miles (24 km) of Saigon. Again and again, ARVN determination

Losses	
NVA:	10,000 killed, 15,000 wounded
ARVN:	2,300 killed/missing, 3,100 wounded

ARMOR AT THE READY
ARVN M-48 Patton tanks are positioned to counter the NVA invasion in 1972. These medium tanks had lighter guns and thinner armor than the Soviet T-54 battle tank used by the NVA, but U.S. supportive air power could defeat even the best enemy armor.

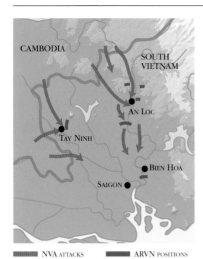

NVA ATTACKS   ARVN POSITIONS

THREATENING THE CAPITAL
NVA invaders from Cambodia came close to breaking through and attacking Saigon in their spring offensive of 1972. Determined ARVN defenders and U.S. air strikes slowed, then turned back the offensive.

and U.S. bombing blunted NVA attacks, which continued to the middle of May. The ARVN then went on the offensive with counterattacks that finally relieved An Loc in mid-July.

As South Vietnam regained much lost ground, ARVN forces proved they could fight well. The Communists held on to Loc Ninh, which they made the temporary VC seat of government. The Communists had taken considerable South Vietnamese territory with the Eastertide Offensive, but their losses had been great. More than 100,000 of the 200,000-man invasion force were casualties, and half their tanks and heavy artillery were destroyed. NVA losses were so heavy that the next NVA invasion would not be until 1975.

Hanoi decided General Giap's field leadership now should end, and he was quietly replaced.

THE LEADERSHIP

AFTER THE FAILURE OF THE Eastertide Offensive, Giap was replaced by General Van Tien Dung. Dung led the effort to make the NVA a conventional army, and commanded the 1975 NVA offensive that defeated South Vietnam.

LE DUAN (1907–1986)
Secretary of Hanoi's committee directing the insurgency in South Vietnam, Le Duan was a major force in the Communist Party. He pushed hard for continuing to fight militarily for reunification of the two Vietnams.

"During the war, we lived close to people, lived in people's hearts."
—Duong Quynh Hoa, a founding member of the NLF

JAMES F. HOLLINGSWORTH (born 1918)
General Hollingsworth planned the air strikes that shattered enemy attacks on An Loc. A former commander of the U.S. First Infantry Division, Hollingsworth was serving as senior adviser to the ARVN III Corps. His motto was: "Kill Cong!"

"The B-52 has become the most effective weapon we have been able to muster."
—Army general John R. McGiffert, on blunting the 1972 invasion

BOMBED AS NEVER BEFORE

To punish Hanoi for its Eastertide invasions, President Nixon ordered bombing of military sites in North Vietnam's territory just north of the DMZ. Although there were only a few thousand U.S. combat troops left in Vietnam, American air power was still potent. More than 1,000 fighter-bombers and 200 B-52 heavy bombers were available. Hanoi continued its offensives in spite of the bombing. Nixon ordered Operation Linebacker— bombing above the 20th parallel.

Now that North Vietnam's field force was becoming a conventional army, it needed supply depots, rail yards, manufacturing, and storage facilities. These made good targets for U.S. bombing. Beginning in May, the industrial port of Haiphong was hit, as were key road and rail bridges. Fighter-bombers used the new laser-guided "smart" bombs to help destroy bridges. Sea mines were dropped in North Vietnamese harbors to threaten shipping. These floating mines blew up if vessels ran into them.

The Paris Peace Talks seemed about to produce an agreement in October, so Nixon called off Linebacker. The negotiations went nowhere, however, because Hanoi refused to agree to Vietnam's being divided. With no settlement, Nixon decided to bomb North Vietnam as never before.

Operation Linebacker II launched devastating B-52 raids on Hanoi and Haiphong between December 18 and 30. This was known as the "Christmas Bombing," although Nixon called a pause for 36 hours over Christmas. The destruction soon resumed. NVA antiaircraft defenses shot down 26 aircraft, including 15 B-52s, but had to fire all their surface-to-air missiles. Without missiles, Hanoi was defenseless against future air attacks.

LINEBACKER STRIKE
The Ninh Binh railroad and highway bridge collapsed into the water after a Navy warplane hit it with a laser-guided bomb. The raid occurred in Than Hoa, near the coast south of Hanoi, in July 1972.

Losses	Linebacker II
U.S.:	26 aircraft lost
North Vietnam:	1,623 civilians killed

On December 30, Nixon called a halt to bombing above the 20th parallel. More than 200,000 tons (180 million kg) of bombs had been dropped.

North Vietnam had suffered heavier bombing in those 13 days than in the previous eight years of war. One result was that peace negotiations resumed. An agreement for a cease-fire to end the fighting was signed on January 27, 1973.

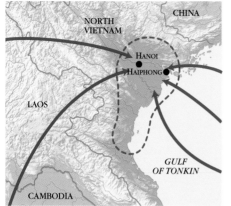

CONVERGING ATTACKS
U.S. heavy bombers and fighter-bombers flew from bases in South Vietnam, Thailand, and from airfields on Pacific islands. Between May and October 1972, Linebacker I sent 41,000 sorties against North Vietnam.

■ ■ ■ ■ APPROXIMATE AREA OF SAM COVER

▬▬▬ U.S. AIR OPERATIONS,
DECEMBER 18–29, 1972

THE LEADERSHIP

THE OUTCOME OF THE WAR now depended on politicians. Nixon wanted Hanoi to stop hostilities, but North Vietnamese leaders—such as Prime Minister Pham Van Dong and Le Duan—were determined to reunify Vietnam.

LE DUC THO (1910–1990)
Tho was one of Hanoi's highest-ranking Communist Party members. From 1970 on, he and U.S. negotiator Henry Kissinger held secret discussions that resulted in the 1973 cease-fire agreements. He declined the Nobel Peace Prize that he and Kissinger were awarded.

"Our troops were exhausted, and… we had not been able to make up our losses."
—Communist general Tran Van Tra, after the 1972 offensive

JOHN D. RYAN (1915–1983)
General Ryan became commander in chief of the U.S. Air Force in 1969. A World War II veteran skilled in strategic bombing, Ryan oversaw the Linebacker I and II attacks on North Vietnam. He retired in 1973.

"[The North Vietnamese] have never been bombed like they're going to be bombed this time."
—Nixon, in the spring of 1972

Third Indochina War, Fall of South Vietnam

The United States, North Vietnam, South Vietnam, and the National Liberation Front agreed to a cease-fire in 1973. The government in Hanoi, however, still wanted reunification.

Cease-fire terms permitted the NVA and VC to remain "in place" in South Vietnam. Neither side was allowed to take new territory, but both Communists and ARVN launched small operations. President Nixon promised President Thieu that South Vietnam would be protected by U.S. air power.

Then Nixon's political career was shattered by scandal in 1974, and he resigned. Vice President Gerald R. Ford became president in August, with a Congress that opposed major military aid to South Vietnam. A few weeks later, Hanoi launched an attack from Cambodia. When the United States did not reply with air strikes, the Communists had their opening. They knew this was the moment to attack,

THE NEW INVADER
Saigon has seen the troops of many armies parading down its streets: Chinese, Japanese, British, French, and American. On April 30, 1975, war-weary residents pause as the latest army, composed of NVA soldiers, marches through the captured city.

August 1974	October	November	December
President Nixon resigns Gerald R. Ford becomes president	North Vietnamese leaders hold a meeting to plan the Ho Chi Minh Campaign	Lieutenant William Calley, responsible for the My Lai massacre, is set free	NVA attacks Phuoc Long

and the Third Indochina War began. A swift Communist campaign overran South Vietnam.

President Ford said publicly the United States could not refight "a war that is finished as far as America is concerned." As the situation grew worse, Ford attempted to get $722 million in emergency aid for South Vietnam. Congress agreed to only $300 million—to evacuate Americans and for humanitarian purposes.

Saigon's fall in April 1975 closed almost 30 years of bitter, bloody warfare. North and South Vietnam were united as the Socialist Republic of Vietnam, with Hanoi the capital. Saigon was renamed Ho Chi Minh City.

The Vietnam War cost the lives of an estimated one million Vietnamese and more than 58,000 Americans.

TANKS AT THE PALACE
It was a well-equipped and modern conventional army—not ragged guerrillas—that finally won this "people's war," as the Communists called the conflict. Soviet-supplied NVA armor drives through the undefended gates of the presidential palace in Saigon on April 30, 1975.

THE REFUGEES

During the war, South Vietnamese fled to the cities to escape fighting in their villages. One-eighth of the population was displaced. South Vietnam's collapse brought about a refugee crisis. One million people tried to escape the country by taking to the open sea, often in small fishing boats. More than 200,000 men, women, and children drowned or died of exposure in the South China Sea. If they survived, the "boat people" were sent to refugee camps in countries where they landed. The United States has accepted 700,000 refugees from Indochina since 1975.

PANIC AND VIOLENCE
These scenes were too common in the last days of South Vietnam as people tried to escape Communist rule. An American official punches a man trying to board an already overloaded aircraft.

January 1975	March	April	April (continued)
President Ford says U.S. will not send military support to South Vietnam	NVA begins final offensive	South Vietnamese president Nguyen Van Thieu resigns and flees the country Duong Van Minh becomes president of South Vietnam	U.S. Embassy evacuated NVA enters presidential palace in Saigon

HANOI RETURNS TO WAR

President Nixon promised to defend South Vietnam if Hanoi violated the 1973 Paris Peace Accords. By 1974, Nixon had resigned. New president Gerald R. Ford and the Congress opposed returning to Vietnam. Military aid began to be reduced. There was no certainty of peace in South Vietnam's future.

President Thieu's government in Saigon had a powerful military—on paper. The ARVN numbered one million men, but they were spread thin, trying to defend too much territory. And both the South Vietnamese government and military were undermined by corruption and bribery. The ARVN was not as strong as it should have been.

By 1974, Hanoi's bomb-shattered industry was slowly getting back on its feet. Also, its forces had recovered from the losses of the 1972 Easter Offensive. Infiltration of supplies and troops continued down the Ho Chi Minh Trail, which by now was a paved highway. Communist fighters in South Vietnam numbered 230,000, with 150,000 of them NVA. The Communists were outnumbered by the ARVN, but Hanoi could choose where to strike. If it did, would the United States return?

On December 13, 1974, Hanoi tested the ARVN's will to fight and the United States' will to respond. Remote,

ARVN BOMBS

A South Vietnamese soldier watches government warplanes bomb enemy positions in January 1975. NVA artillery was more potent, however. It fired 3,000 rounds a day on ARVN troops holding the air base at Song Be, near Phuoc Long City.

Losses	
NVA:	unknown
ARVN:	4,550 killed

lightly defended Phuoc Long Province was the first objective. Two NVA divisions and a battalion of Soviet-built tanks overran the mainly militia and home-guard forces. ARVN reinforcements rushed in but could not match the attackers' firepower. Phuoc Long City fell on January 8.

When the United States did not even send air support to try to prevent the fall of Phuoc Long, it was clear that the war was now a Vietnamese struggle. Hanoi prepared to launch the "final campaign" for all South Vietnam.

PHUOC LONG
Overwhelming NVA forces attacked Phuoc Long Province in December 1974. An ARVN infantry battalion with six artillery pieces was helilifted to Phuoc Long City. It was wiped out.

▰▰▰▰ NVA ATTACKS
▰▰▰▰ ARVN AIR ASSAULTS
▪▪▪▪ ARVN RETREAT

Communist planners expected it to take two years. They did not know how weak Thieu's government really was.

THE LEADERSHIP

By 1975, Hanoi's high command was led by a new generation of officers. General Van Tien Dung commanded the drive to capture Saigon. President Thieu's South Vietnamese generals were hampered by deep cuts in U.S. aid in 1974.

"Now they need that helping hand more than ever."
—General Weyand, calling for aid to South Vietnam

NGUYEN CAO KY (born 1930)
General Ky was a dashing South Vietnamese fighter pilot and a leader of the air force. He served as RVN premier in President Thieu's government from 1965 to 1971. Ky escaped to the United States after the war.

"We had to conduct large-scale… battles to destroy…the enemy."
—Hanoi's General Dung, planning for the final campaign

NGUYEN DUY TRINH (1910-1985)
Trinh was deputy prime minister and foreign minister for North Vietnam and later the unified Socialist Republic of Vietnam from 1965 to 1980. He served in southern Vietnam as a Vietminh leader during the First Indochina War. Trinh signed the Paris Peace Accords.

SUDDEN DEFEAT

The Communists pushed their offensive, striking through the Central Highlands in March. Many ARVN units fought hard, but they were driven steadily back toward the seacoast. From Saigon, Thieu desperately gave his generals orders that could not be obeyed because of rapid Communist advances. Hué fell on March 26, and Da Nang on March 30. Thousands of ARVN soldiers and refugees were evacuated by sea. Millions more South Vietnamese civilians crowded the roads, trying to escape the fighting. The NVA swept down from the DMZ and attacked from Cambodian border bases.

Hanoi called this final push the "Ho Chi Minh Campaign."

President Ford announced that the United States would not be drawn back into the conflict. ARVN morale was weakened by this position. Without United States intervention, the door was open for Hanoi's triumph. Yet, while some ARVN forces fled, others fought stubbornly.

The ARVN Eighteenth Division stood fast at Xuan Loc, 45 miles (75 km) east of Saigon. This mix of soldiers and militia was led by General Le Minh Dao. It came under massive artillery barrages on April 9, followed by armor attacks. NVA assaults were repulsed with heavy loss. Three days of fighting later, the Eighteenth was reinforced and held on for two more weeks. At least 5,000 Communists were killed, and

Losses Xuan Loc	
NVA:	5,000 killed/wounded
ARVN:	unknown

DESPERATE TO ESCAPE
Civilians flee from the fighting around Saigon in April 1975. A roadblock is cleared for anxious South Vietnamese packed into automobiles and trucks and riding motorbikes. Many would continue their journey on the bicycles loaded onto vehicles.

37 NVA tanks destroyed. The Eighteenth Division suffered 30 percent casualties. On April 22, the defenders evacuated Xuan Loc after again proving the valor of well-led South Vietnamese troops.

U.S. military historian General Phillip B. Davidson described Xuan Loc as "one of the epic battles of any of the Indochina wars, certainly the most heroic stand in Indochina War III."

Now the NVA columns drove toward the capital, Saigon, which was being encircled. The U.S. Embassy staff was still in the city. American diplomats had not expected the enemy offensive to be so swift.

On April 21, President Thieu resigned and fled the country.

LIGHTNING CAMPAIGN
"Lightning speed!" General Dung ordered as his forces rolled through South Vietnam. All columns drove for Saigon, the seat of government.

THE LEADERSHIP

WHEN PRESIDENT THIEU TRIED TO COMMAND ARVN forces himself in the field, his incompetence caused more defeats. Some ARVN generals fled, abandoning their troops. Others, such as General Truong, stayed with their men. Truong evacuated Da Nang by sea.

NGUYEN THANH TRUNG (born 1948)
An RVN Air Force lieutenant, Trung turned against his government on April 8, 1975, and bombed Saigon's presidential palace. He was a secret Communist agent. Trung took his fighter to a VC base and later flew for Hanoi.

"The United States has not respected its promises. It is not trustworthy."
—President Thieu, upon resigning, April 21, 1975

VAN TIEN DUNG (1917-2002)
NVA commander in chief since 1953, General Dung was one of the few true peasants in the Communist leadership. He was close to Giap and fought at Dien Bien Phu. Dung took personal command of the conquest of South Vietnam.

"The failure to support South Vietnam [is] a failure of a moral commitment of the United States."
—Defense Secretary James Schlesinger

COMMUNISTS TRIUMPH

No one, including officials in Hanoi, expected the North Vietnamese campaign to move so fast. General Van Tien Dung was eager to attack Saigon. If the monsoon rains came before he attacked, the mud would be impassable for armored tanks. Also, Thieu would have more time to regroup his forces and fight on. Or he might persuade the Americans to send air support.

Massive bombing would slow the Communist advance, but Congress opposed such a step. Instead, all nonessential Americans, U.S. employees, and dependents, were told to fly to safety immediately.

On April 21, Thieu resigned and fled the country. His vice president, Tran Van Huong, turned over leadership to retired ARVN general Duong Van Minh. Hoping he could negotiate with the Communists, Minh accepted the presidency. Hanoi would accept no terms, however—no conditions.

The courageous ARVN Eighteenth Division was overrun defending Bien Hoa air base, and a savage tank battle raged at Long Thanh. The NVA closed in. When the encirclement of Saigon was complete, Dung briefly paused to see whether the RVN government would collapse. Then, on April 27, he launched a rocket barrage and warplane strikes. This made it impossible for the remaining American evacuees to get out by airplane.

Marine helicopters came to the rescue, carrying almost 4,400 people to carriers off shore. Confusion led to more problems at the U.S. Embassy,

FLIGHT TO SAFETY
A CIA helicopter takes on Americans and foreign nationals escaping Saigon on April 29, 1975. This was just one day before the city surrendered. The chopper has landed on the tiny roof of a building near the U.S. Embassy.

Statistics
Following the fall of Saigon 675,000 refugees are evacuated to the United States

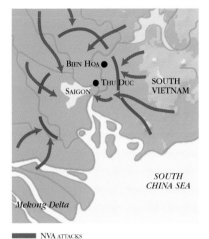

NVA ATTACKS
ARVN DEFENSIVE LINES

BATTLE FOR SAIGON

Overwhelming military might shattered the ARVN defenders around Saigon. The assault lasted from April 27 to April 30, when the Republic of South Vietnam's government surrendered unconditionally to the Communists.

where 3,000 people appeared instead of the expected 100 evacuees. Helicopters again went to work. This evacuation ended by dawn on April 30, but miscommunication resulted in more than 400 people being left behind.

Around noon, NVA tanks rumbled through the gates of the presidential palace, and President Minh surrendered. The war was over.

THE LEADERSHIP

Two DIVISIONS IN THE CAMPAIGN were led by Communist general Tran Van Tra. Many ARVN field commanders had fled or surrendered. Two ARVN generals, Nguyen Khoa Nam and Le Van Hung, committed suicide. Ambassador Graham Martin was one of the last Americans to leave.

DUONG VAN MINH (1916–2001)
While commanding RVN forces in 1963, Minh led the coup that overthrew Diem. Soon overthrown himself, Minh was exiled for four years. He again became president upon Thieu's resignation in April 1975. Minh emigrated to France in 1983.

"Remain calm, stop fighting, and stay put."
—Minh's orders to his forces, April 30, 1975

GERALD R. FORD (born 1913)
Ford replaced Nixon as president in August 1974. U.S. forces had been withdrawn, and Congress disliked spending too much on South Vietnam. When Ford did not send bombers to oppose the Phuoc Long offensive, Hanoi knew it could continue the campaign.

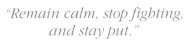

"Attack Saigon now when the enemy, in utter disarray, has lost his strength."
—Le Duc Tho, former peace negotiator for Hanoi

GENERALS AND PARTY LEADERS

COMMUNIST LEADERS

VO CHI CONG
Chairman of the NLF and
chief political officer; chief
of state, Socialist Republic
of Vietnam, 1987–91

NGUYEN THI DINH
Leading revolutionary leader,
1940s–1975; deputy
commander of the NLF
armed forces, Viet Cong

NGUYEN VAN HIEU
General secretary of NLF,
1960; minister of culture
and information, Socialist
Republic of Vietnam

DUONG QUYNH HOA
Medical doctor; founding
member of the NLF; prominent
critic of the Socialist Republic
of Vietnam after the war

NGUYEN LE THAN
Spokesman for North
Vietnamese delegation
at Paris Peace Talks

TRUONG NHU TANG
A founder of the NLF; became
disillusioned with Socialist
Republic of Vietnam after the
war; exiled to France

NGUYEN DUY TRINH
Member Indochinese
Communist Party, 1920s; fought
French in First Indochina War;
DRV foreign minister, 1965–80;
held high positions in DRV

TRAN NAM TRUNG
Fought French in First
Indochina War; imprisoned
by French; commander
of the NLF armed forces,
Viet Cong

THUY XUAN
Imprisoned by French, 1939–45;
DRV foreign minister,
1963–65; North Vietnamese
peace negotiator during Paris
Peace Accords, 1973

"This is [not a jungle war, but] a struggle for freedom on every front of human activity."

—President Lyndon B. Johnson, 1964

ALLIED LEADERS

NGUYEN VAN CHUAN
French military academy;
commanded the ARVN
First Division Infantry;
Commander I Corps, 1966

ROBERT E. CUSHMAN
Annapolis; World War II;
commander III Marine
Amphibious Force 1967–69;
oversaw defense of Khe Sanh

NGUYEN VAN DIEM
Lieutenant colonel in the
ARVN forces; commanded First
Regiment, ARVN First Division,
the elite Ben Hai regiment

NGO DZU
Commander II Corps, 1970–72;
worked closely with U.S.
advisor John Paul Vann during
1972 Eastertide Offensive

JEAN E. ENGLER
West Point; World War II;
deputy commander MACV,
1966; deputy chief of staff
for logistics, 1967–69

HAROLD K. JOHNSON
West Point; World War II;
survived Bataan Death March;
Korean War; army chief
of staff, 1964–68

MELVIN LAIRD
Secretary of defense, 1969–73;
architect of "Vietnamization"
to improve the ARVN forces;
advocated U.S. troop
withdrawals

CURTIS LEMAY
Air force chief of staff
1961–65; World War II;
said U.S. should "bomb
[North Vietnam] back
to the Stone Age"

JOHN P. MCCONNELL
West Point; World War II; air
force chief of staff, 1965–69;
advocated heavier bombing
of North Vietnam to
achieve victory

ALLIED LEADERS

HENRI NAVARRE
French commander in chief
of combined forces in
Indochina, 1953–54; defeated
at Dien Bien Phu

JOHN O'DANIEL
"Iron Mike"; army general;
chief of Military Assistance
Advisory Group-Indochina
(MAAG-I), 1954–56

WILLIAM ROGERS
Secretary of state 1969–73;
opposed Operation Menu,
Cambodia invasion; supported
"Vietnamization"

WILLIAM B. ROSSON
West Point; World
War II; military
advisor during First
Indochina War;
commanded Task
Force Oregon; deputy
commander MACV

CHARLES J. TIMMES
Chief, Military
Assistance Advisory
Group (MAAG) 1962;
quoted in *NY Times*,
1962, "We are now
doing a little better
than holding our own."

THOMAS J.H. TRAPNELL
West Point; World War II;
survived Bataan Death March;
Korea; commander MAAG,
Vietnam, 1952–53

LEWIS W. WALT
Marine general; World War
II, Korean War; senior
advisor to and coordinator
of South Vietnam's I Corps

SAMUEL T. WILLIAMS
Army general; commanded
MAAG, Vietnam, 1955–60;
called for increase in number
of U.S. advisors in Vietnam

EARL G. WHEELER
West Point; army
chief of staff,
1962–64; chairman
of the Joint Chiefs
of Staff, 1964–70

ELMO R. ZUMWALT JR.
Annapolis; World
War II; admiral;
commander U.S.
Naval Forces,
Vietnam, 1968–70

INDEX

A–C

Abrams, Creighton W., 66–69
Acheson, Dean, 6
Agent Orange, 43
An Khe, 39
An Loc, Battle of, 79, 80–81
Ap Bac, Battle of, 21, 24–25
Ap Bia Mountain, 67, 69
A Shau Valley, 69
Australian forces, 42–44
Bao Dai, 6–9, 16–17, 22
Bien Hoa Airfield, 91
Brown Water Navy, 67
Bui Tin, 65
Calley, William, 67
Cambodia, 12, 17, 26–27, 38, 43, 51–52, 68, 70–75, 80–81, 88–89
Cambodia, Invasion of, 68, 70–75
Cam Ranh Bay, 12, 36, 42
Castries, Christian de, 18–19
Central Intelligence Agency (CIA), 22, 64–65
Central Office for South Vietnam (COSVN), 51
Cheatham, Ernest C., 58–59
China, People's Republic of, 6–7, 17–19, 76
"Christmas Bombing," 83
Chu Huy Man, 38–41
Coastal Surveillance Force, 36–37
Coast Guard, 36–37
Colby, William E., 64–65
Con Thien, 52
CORDS (Civilian Operations and Revolutionary Development), 64–65
Cushman, Robert E., 93

D–G

Dak To, Battle of, 47, 52–53
Da Nang, 12, 30–31, 88
Davidson, Phillip B., 53, 74, 89
Desoto Patrol, 29
Destroyer Division, 192, 29
Do Cao Tri, 73
Dong Si Nguyen, 27
Demilitarized Zone (DMZ), 12
Ngo Dinh Diem, 7–9, 20–25, 28, 35
Dien Bien Phu, Battle of, 14–19, 60, 89
Duong Quynh Hoa, 92
Duong Van Minh, 90–91
Eastertide Offensive, 76, 78–83
Eighteenth Infantry Division (ARVN), 88–89
Eighth Tactical Fighter Wing, 48
Eighty-second Airborne Division, 45
Eisenhower, Dwight D., 6–7, 20, 22
Engler, Jean E., 93
Enterprise, USS, 43
"Fishhook," 72–73

Fifth Marine Regiment, 59
First Cavalry Div., 9, 38–42, 61
I Field Force, 53
First Indochina War, 6–19, 31, 35
First Infantry Division, 51
First Infantry Division (ARVN), 78
503rd Airborne Regiment, 53
Ford, Gerald R., 84–86, 88, 90–91
Fourth Infantry Division, 52–53
France, 6–19, 26, 91
Free World Military Forces, 44
Galloway, Joseph, 41
Geneva Convention (1949), 77
Geneva Accords, 19
Group 559, 26–27
Gulf of Tonkin Incident, 21, 28–29, 32
Gulf of Tonkin Resolution, 29–30, 71

H–J

Haig, Alexander M., 50
Hamburger Hill, Battle of, 69
Hanoi, 9, 32, 48, 65, 76–78, 81–91
Haiphong, 32, 48, 77, 82–83
Harkins, Paul D., 22, 27
Harrington, Myron, 57
Herrick, John J., 29
Herrington, Stuart, 65
Hill 875, 47, 53
Hoang Xuan Lam, 74–75
Ho Chi Minh, 6–7, 14–19, 29–33, 67
Ho Chi Minh Campaign, 88–89
Ho Chi Minh Trail, 32, 37–38, 68, 74, 86
Hoffman, Carl W., 62
Hollingsworth, James F., 80–81
Honeycutt, Weldon, 69
Howze, Hamilton, 39
Hué, Battle of, 58–59, 74
Huynh Van Cao, 24–25
Ia Drang, Battle of, 31, 38–41
Iron Triangle, 45, 50
Jackson, O.D., 44
Jackson State, 70–71
Jacobssen, George Jr., 33
Japan, 14–16
Johnson, Harold K., 93
Johnson, James H., 53
Johnson, Lyndon B., 8–9, 21, 28–35, 42, 48
Johnson, Richard H., 53

K–L

Kennedy, John F., 8–9, 20–25
Kent State University, 70–71
Khe Sanh, Siege of, 52, 57, 62–63
Khmer Rouge, 70–71, 72–75
Kinnard, Harry W.O., 38–40
Kissinger, Henry, 76, 83
Komer, Robert W., 64–65
Kontum, 79

Korean War, 17, 35, 41, 51
Lahue, Foster C., 58
Laird, Melvin R., 93
Lam Son 719, 74–75
Landsdale, Edward, 22
Laos, 12, 17, 26–27, 43, 47, 52, 69, 74–75
Lattre de Tassigny, Jean de, 16–17
Le Duan, 67, 80–81, 83
Le Duc Tho, 76, 82–83, 91
LeMay, Curtis E., 93
Le Minh Dao, 88
Le Van Hung, 91
Le Van Than, 58
Linebacker I and II, 76–77, 82–83
Loc Ninh, 80–81
Lodge, Henry C., 22
Long Binh, 60–61, 64
Long Tan, Battle of, 43–44
Lon Nol, 72–73
Lownds, David, 62–63
Loyalty, USS, 36
LZ Albany, Battle of, 40–41
LZ X-Ray, Battle of, 40–41

M–N

Maddox, USS, 28–29
Mao Zedong, 6–7, 17
Martin, Graham, 91
McConnell, John P., 93
McElroy, John W., 62
McKeown, Alfred H., 23
McNamara Robert S., 32, 39, 49
MEDEVAC, 75
Mekong Delta, 24, 64–66
Meloy, Guy S., 45
Military Assistance Advisory Group (MAAG), 22
Military Assistance Command, Vietnam (MACV), 12, 34–35, 53, 55, 60–63, 66, 68
Momyer, William, 33
Montagnards, 39
Moore, Harold G., 39–41
My Lai Massacre, 66–67
National Liberation Front, 21, 37, 84
Naval Forces, Vietnam, 37
Navarre, Henri, 18–19, 94
New York, 47
Ngo Dinh Diem, 20–23
Ngo Dzu, 93
Ngo Quang Truong, 58, 78–79, 88–89
Nguyen Cao Ky, 86–87
Nguyen Khoa Nam, 91
Nguyen Duy Trinh, 86–87, 92
Nguyen Huu An, 40–41, 53
Nguyen Huu Tho, 35
Nguyen Le Than, 92
Nguyen Thanh Trung, 89
Nguyen Thi Binh, 37
Nguyen Thi Dinh, 92
Nguyen Van Chuan, 93
Nguyen Van Diem, 93
Nguyen Van Hieu, 92

ACKNOWLEDGMENTS
Media Projects, Inc., and DK Publishing, Inc., offer their grateful thanks to: Clifford J. Rogers, Associate Professor of History, United States Military Academy; Steve R. Waddell, Associate Professor of History, United States Military Academy; Erika Rubel; Walter H. Bradford, Pablo Jimenez-Reyes (for photography), Marc W. Sammis, and Mike Valdez of the U.S. Army Center of Military History; Jeremy Murray; Timothy Murray; Jemal Creary, Donna Daley, Dina Keil, Mary Luhrs, Marc Rampulla, and Robinya Roberts of the Corbis/UPI research team; Ron Toelke for cartography; Rob Stokes for relief mapping.

Photography and Art Credits
(t=top; b=bottom; l=left; r=right; c=center; a=above)
© **Alinari Archives/CORBIS:** 14tr, 14–15b.
© **Bettmann/CORBIS:** 6t, 7t, 8t, 9t, 9b, 11bl, 17cl, 20tr, 21cr, 22br, 23b, 24b, 25br, 27cl, 29cl, 33cl, 42–43b, 42t, 43cr, 54t, 66–67b, 66t, 67cr, 70–71b, 75b, 76–77b, 76tr, 83br, 85cr, 90b, 91br, 92bl, 92br, 92c, 92tl, 92tc, 92tr, 92bc.
© **CORBIS:** 77cr. © **Francoise de Mulder/CORBIS:** 73cl, 84–85b, 84tr. © **Nik Wheeler/CORBIS:** 88b.

© **Royalty-Free/CORBIS:** 39cl, 41cl, 53b. © **Tim Page/CORBIS:** 1, 30–31b, 30t, 44br, 64b. © **Wally McNamee/CORBIS:** 65cl. **Associated Press Photo from New York (Photographer John Filo):** 70t. **United States Army Center of Military History:** 4t, 4b, 5cl, 5cr, 36c, 51cr, 59c, 63c, 64c, 72c, 75c. **Library of Congress:** 73cl. **National Archives:** 2–3, 6b, 7b, 8b, 9c, 10cl, 10tr, 11tl, 11cr, 15cr, 16b, 18br, 19b, 20–21b, 22cl, 26b, 27br, 28b, 29br, 32b, 34b, 35br, 36b, 37cl, 37br, 38b, 40b, 44cl, 45cl, 45br, 46t, 46–47b, 47cr, 48b, 49cl, 49br, 50cl, 50br, 51cl, 51br, 52b, 53cl, 54–55b, 55cr, 56cl, 56br, 57b, 58cl, 58br, 59b, 60cl, 60br, 61b, 62cl, 62br, 63b, 65br, 68cl, 68br, 69cl, 69br, 71cr, 72b, 74cl, 74br 78cl, 78br, 79b, 80b, 81br, 87cl, 87br, 89cl, 89br, 91cl, 93tl, 93tc, 93tr, 93c, 93cr, 93bl, 93br, 94tr, 94cla, 94cra, 94clb, 94cb, 94crb, 94bl, 94br. **United Press International/CORBIS:** 17br, 18cl, 25cl, 31cr, 33cl, 35cl, 39br, 41br, 81cl, 82b, 83cl, 86b, 92cl, 92cr, 93cl, 93bc, 94tl, 94tc.

Cover Credits: © **Bettmann/CORBIS:** front t, front cr, front bl, front br, front flap, back. © **Joseph Sohm; ChromoSohm Inc./CORBIS:** front ca © **Nik Wheeler/CORBIS:** front cb.